Vietnam is famous for a long, protracted war that left many with a scar yet unhealed. What you don't know about Vietnam is the life and work of Southern Baptist missionaries in that land of conflict. Sam Jam~~ ~~ oura-geous souls who risked everything t~ ~ ~ story and thus reveals the heart of a peop ook should have a life of its own among !l their defining life experience. He describ~ ~als the difficulties of living cross-culturally ~ing theme of victory in Jesus. I cannot re ~ ~ window on the world through the eyes of a se~

> —L. Russ Bush, Academic Dean
> Southeastern Baptist Theological Seminary

Those of us who have known and worked with Sam James have been blessed to benefit from his sensitive counsel and insights gained from more than 40 years of mission-field experiences and leadership roles. His leadership and understanding of missions has nothing theoretical about it. In this volume Dr. James captures in graphic reality the challenges of cross-cultural witness in a dangerous and hostile environment. Every missionary and missionary candidate would benefit from reading this testimony of dedication, devotion, and sacrifice and the faithfulness of God's power and providence.

> —Jerry Rankin, President
> International Mission Board, SBC

If you love adventure, missions, and real-life stories, this is the book for you. Sam James truly was God's servant on the edge of history in war-torn Vietnam. He and his family laid their lives on the line every day for the cause of Christ. You will feel his personality, convictions, and faith in God in these thrilling stories of God at work on the edge of the Great Commission. You will want to share with others these stories of love, danger, fear, grief, joy, and the miraculous intervention of God.

> —Avery Willis, Emeritus Senior Vice-President for Overseas Operations
> International Mission Board, SBC

Sam James is a missionary extraordinaire, but the God he serves is the One he puts in the spotlight. In reading his book I feel as though I have been to Vietnam. Through it I have met some new brothers in Christ, almost tasted the food, seen the sights, and been on the "inside" of a devoted missionary and his family. The greatest joy in reading this book was hearing how a number of individuals trusted Christ and the careful giving of credit and glory to the Lord. The insights into culture and decision-making will be a significant aid to my students as they look forward to international missions.

> —John Floyd, Administrative Vice-President
> Director of the Doctor of Ministry Program, Professor of Missions
> Mid-America Baptist Theological Seminary

Want to make missions personal? Then read *Servant on the Edge of History: Risking All for the Gospel in War-Ravaged Vietnam.* This is a book that brings the impact of missions past your doorstep and into your heart. The author's wealth of experience, animated writing, and affable personality are combined to reveal an underlying passion for the spread of the gospel under the most difficult of circumstances. Each chapter is a stand-alone, true-life account of the impact of the gospel on the lives of people who risked all in the expression of their faith. Combined, they leave the reader with an overwhelming sense of the sufficiency of Christ and a sense of urgency in spreading the gospel. Don't read this book unless you are prepared to have your life permanently marked for missions!

—*Tom Eliff, Senior Pastor*
First Baptist Church, Del City, OK

SERVANT

ON THE

EDGE OF HISTORY

Risking All for the Gospel
in War-Ravaged Vietnam

SAM JAMES

Foreword by Henry Blackaby

✝HANNIBAL BOOKS
www.hannibalbooks.com

Printed in the United States of America
by Versa Press, East Peoria, IL
Cover design by Greg Crull
Except where otherwise indicated, Scripture taken
from the NEW AMERICAN STANDARD BIBLE, Copyright
1960, 1962, 1963, 1968, 1971, 1972, 1973, 1975, 1977, by the
Lockman Foundation. Used by permission.
Library of Congress Control Number: 2005933237
ISBN 0-929292-66-9

Hannibal Books
P.O. Box 461592
Garland, Texas 75046
1-800-747-0738
www.hannibalbooks.com

On the cover: Tragic aftermath of the Tet Offensive, Saigon,
February, 1968.

Dedication

This book, above all, is dedicated to Rachel, my wife,
who to me has been the very essence of God's love
and has shared intimately in every story told in this book.

It is dedicated to four of the most wonderful and committed
children any father and mother could ever have—
Deborah, Stephen, Philip, and Michael.
Through more than four decades of missionary service
they have never once questioned our call to serve overseas.
To the contrary they always have shared in that call and participated
in our ministry. My family has been an inspiration to me
and has kept me going even when continuing
to do so seemed impossible.

I also dedicate this book to the hundreds of missionaries all over the
world who encouraged the writing of these stories and who gave
affirmation and inspiration through these many years.

This book is also dedicated to John McGill,
of Wallace Memorial Baptist Church in Knoxville, TN,
who believed in the value of this book and helped to bring it into
being. His personal involvement gave the needed impetus
and inspiration to complete the writing.

Contents

Foreword

For years Sam James has been a true "missionary hero" to me. He never would accept this description. But he, along with his wife, Rachel, thoroughly deserve it. They served at the clear call of God, but the living out in real life and in real situations awaited them. Sam has thoroughly captured in writing the God-initiated moments when God made him into an "authentic missionary." He has incredibly taken us into most all of the biblical, then practical, decisions that must be faced and made with integrity before God and men. In the process he captures the deep and real dilemmas of extremes in every decision that grows out of real situations and arrives at a biblically authentic balance in his own response. In so doing he makes us "live out" with him the inner struggles of living the missionary call. These are brilliantly conveyed in his writing.

I've been in many of these places; I bear witness that Sam accurately has described his soul transparently before God Who called him and Rachel to be God's chosen and called servants in an unusually hostile environment—the war that raged in Vietnam.

His heart to engage all believers with God in a broken and heartbreaking world is exceptional, as he concludes each chapter with a summary and vital questions for our lives.

Sam has captured deeply what James said about faith: "faith without works is dead" (Jas. 2:20, NKJV). But he effectively has demonstrated further what James wrote: " . . . faith was working together with his works, and by works faith was made perfect (complete) . . . " (Jas. 2:22, NKJV). Correct theology is good. But faith must be completed by works—lived out and made real in the broken world where He's assigned us. This book is essential for all active missionaries, whatever their base is, and for every leader— yes, and every serious believer in Christ!

Henry T. Blackaby; Author, *Experiencing God*
President, Henry Blackaby Ministries

Introduction

This book is set in Vietnam. The events occurred during the trauma of trying to be a servant of the Lord in an environment permeated with the results of war. Reading these stories simply as tales of the Vietnam war would be wrong. These stories are about a few, very average people—the author included—who lived their lives while realizing God's presence and His dynamic intervention at significant moments. These events resulted in new growth and knowledge about Who God is and who a person can be when life is lived consciously in His presence. They are stories about the human experience of fear, of loss, of failure, of success. They are stories about the victory that occurs when Jesus becomes the source of one's life. They are stories about the difference Christ makes in life, especially under traumatic conditions.

While the stories are personal in nature, I have not intended to write an autobiography. The intent is to show how one person grew in his understanding of himself and God through his own human experience and that of other people. These events show the difference Jesus Christ makes in the lives of persons who experience adversity and who arrive at a new meaning in life through it.

The Lord gave one man some wonderful opportunities and experiences from which to gain new insight into Who God is and what life means when lived in the reality of His presence. Just as these form the fabric of the author's life, so are you, the reader, challenged to be open to the potential of living each moment of life as a learner as you walk daily with the Lord. Discover the meaning in those experiences that have the potential of forming the fabric of life that can make you the beautiful person you want to be.

Note that discussion questions appear at the end of chapters. We provide these to enable you to discuss in small-group settings what you have read. If that is not possible, then use the discussion questions in your own thought processes to help you apply to your life the experiences described. May God bless you as you read.

Sam James
Midlothian, VA; September, 2005

Chapter 1

A Meeting at the Zoo

My wife, Rachel, and I looked down from the plane on which we traveled. We viewed green rice paddies and a myriad of canals below. We were making our first trip back to Vietnam after 14 years of absence since our hasty and hazardous exit during the communist takeover in 1975. Bob and Ida Davis, who had served with us as Southern Baptist missionaries in Vietnam, accompanied us.

As we descended toward the airport, the scene below gradually changed from rice paddies and canals to scattered houses, to villages, and finally to the sprawl of Saigon, now renamed Ho Chi Minh City. We had no way of knowing what would happen when we landed at that airport.

We had sent word to some of the Vietnamese Christians with whom we worked in bygone days that we were arriving, but we could not be sure they had received that information. We also did not know if the conditions under the communist government were such that our friends could contact us. We had no way of knowing if, when we reached the immigration desk, our previous years in Vietnam would prevent our entering the country. We feared we might be told to get back on the plane and leave.

My heart beat wildly as I stepped from the plane to board the bus that would take us to the terminal. I looked around the airport at the terminal building and the tarmac from which I had boarded on that fateful April night in 1975, in the hours of the chaotic "fall" of Vietnam. That night I took off in total darkness and did not know whether I would ever return to this land again. That night seemed a lifetime ago. Then my heart raced with fear and anxiety. Today it raced with anticipation and hope.

As we stepped off of the bus to enter the terminal, my attention fell on a huge number of people standing on the roof of the terminal. As we looked more closely, we could see that most of the crowd consisted of our Christian friends. We trembled with excitement as we went through the immigration and customs formalities and prepared to walk out of that building and for the first time in all of those years experience Vietnam again.

As we stepped through the doors, we were met with a crush of Christian friends who greeted us with excited greetings, hugs, and tears of joy. During those long years away from Vietnam I had labored under intense feelings of guilt at having left our Christian people in their darkest hour. I felt like a shepherd who had abandoned his sheep as they faced great danger. I wondered if they harbored ill-will toward me for leaving them so suddenly during those last hours before communist forces entered the city. Now, we were surrounded by those friends who welcomed us back and expressed such love and joy at our return. The government-owned bus waited to take us to our hotel. By the moment the driver grew more impatient and nervous. Finally the security police tore us away from the crowd and physically shoved us into the bus!

Thus began the most exciting and stimulating visit we ever have made anywhere in our lives. Security in 1989 was very tight. Our friends were not able to visit us at our hotel lest the security police call them in for severe questioning. We were not free to visit in their homes. After the greeting at the airport, we were able to have little or no contact with any of them except for worship at the government-recognized Grace Baptist Church on Sunday.

One morning as Bob Davis and I left our hotel, someone—seemingly by accident—bumped into me on the sidewalk. Before I could see who it was, I felt a piece of paper thrust in my hand. As I unfolded it, I read, "Meet us at the zoo at 2 this afternoon." We had no idea who had given me that paper. Was it a government agent who wanted to catch us doing something wrong? Was it one of our former Christians who was setting up a meeting?

After some debate, we decided to take the risk and go to the zoo. Bob and I boarded a "pedicab", the predominant mode of transportation in Vietnamese cities in that day. It is basically a three-wheel bicycle with a seat on the front for the passenger. We arrived at the zoo at 2 p.m. sharp, paid the pedicab driver, and walked toward the zoo entrance. A man standing at the gate motioned for us to follow him. We followed him at a distance through the winding paths deep inside the zoo interior. At one time the Saigon zoo was a beautiful place with a myriad of exotic animals, most of which are native to Vietnam and to the Indo-Chinese peninsula. Now, years of neglect resulted in the zoo becoming a huge jungle with empty cages. Dense undergrowth was everywhere. It even encroached the path where we walked.

Suddenly the man turned off the path into the dense undergrowth. He motioned for us to follow. Again, plunging into that undergrowth and not knowing where we were going or whom we would meet was a big, and somewhat terrifying, decision. We decided that we had traveled this far and simply must proceed on.

We finally stepped into a small clearing. In the middle was an old, rusty, round table and several iron chairs that were rusty but clean enough for someone to sit down. From the surrounding wilderness stepped seven men. Our hearts were in our throats as we pondered who they were and what they wanted with us.

Chapter 2

Beginning with a Miracle

How did all this occur in my life? How had my family happened to be in war-ravaged Vietnam in the first place so many years ago? What events had set in motion our commitment to serve Christ in this foreign land? As my family and I landed in the Republic of South Vietnam on November 9, 1962, at Tan San Nhut Airport near Saigon, I felt certain that this place would be our home for the rest of our lives.

We had waited a long time for this day. In 1955, after my discharge from the United States Navy and having served for four years in the Pacific including in the Korean War, I wrote to the-then Foreign Mission Board (now International Mission Board) of the Southern Baptist Convention. In my letter I expressed my desire to go to Vietnam as a missionary. In the early 1950s, my ship, the U.S.S. Sitkoh Bay, a small aircraft carrier, had made the trip up the Saigon River. Since that time I had been fascinated by Vietnam. A huge magnet had seemed to steadily draw me toward that nation. I remember, just after committing my life completely to Jesus Christ, bowing my head as I stood on the catwalk below the flight deck and looked out across the Asian countryside. In my prayer I asked where He wanted me to serve Him. An almost immediate impression never faded from my thinking. I believed I was to plant my life overseas among people who have little opportunity to learn about Jesus. At this point Vietnam had become the focus of my desire to serve. The reply from the "Secretary for the Orient" at the Foreign Mission Board was that Southern Baptists have no missionaries in Vietnam. Plans at present do not include Vietnam, he wrote. This disappointed me, but the desire continued unabated with intensity throughout my college years at Wake Forest University and my graduate years at Southeastern Baptist Theological Seminary. I was greatly thrilled when in 1959, toward the end of my second year in the seminary, the Foreign Mission Board officially voted to make Vietnam one of its mission fields.

In January 1961, at Gulfshore, MS, my wife, Rachel, and I went through a brief orientation for missionary service. We were to be appointed in March and, on my graduation in May 1961, depart for Vietnam. Our son, Stephen, was born in February with a small physical defect which delayed our appointment. Never once did the call to Vietnam waver, however. One year later, Stephen's defect was corrected by surgery. In March 1962 we were appointed as missionaries to the Republic of South Vietnam.

War clouds already were on the horizon. They were small but potentially ominous. As we stood on the platform on March 7, 1962, for appointment, Dr. Baker James Cauthen, executive secretary of the Foreign Mission Board, said to Rachel and me, "You are going to Vietnam. Things are not looking good there for the future. Take whatever you want to take. Take your piano, your appliances, and anything else you want to take. But take them in your hands. If they ever get into your heart, you are through as a missionary." Dr. and Mrs. Cauthen had lost everything three times in China as they fled the Japanese invasion and later the communist revolution. He spoke from first-hand experience. Little did we know that his words would be prophetic.

We started our missionary service with a miracle and continued witnessing miracle after miracle in our lives. The first miracle after our appointment was that we received permission to enter Vietnam. We arrived in Hong Kong on July 3, 1962, with a daughter, Deborah, 3; a son, Stephen, 18 months; and a son, Philip, 11 weeks. This meant three children in night diapers in a time when disposable diapers hardly were available. We boarded the SS President Wilson for the three-week journey from San Francisco to Hong Kong. We slept in one small stateroom two decks down. Being able to go ashore in Hong Kong after these three weeks at sea was enjoyable beyond description! We had expected our visas for Vietnam to be ready for us on arrival so that we could proceed almost immediately for Vietnam. This was not to be. Our visas were not waiting for us.

We temporarily stayed in a small Chinese hotel as we awaited our visas. We took the small one-and-one-half rooms on the third floor of the Four Seas Hotel on Waterloo Road in Kowloon and began our wait. How challenging to eat every meal in the Chinese dining room with small children who had not yet learned to eat with dignity in a public area! We always had enjoyed Chinese restaurants but never had eaten all of our meals—morning, noon, and night for weeks on end—in one.

Almost immediately Rachel noticed on entry that our hotel room was infested with small green lizards that could walk up and down the walls and across the ceiling without falling. Opening the window curtains was particularly unnerving as the lizards were startled and jumped to the floor in fear. They loved dresser drawers full of underwear, which with every opening precipitated a near heart attack. They loved to congregate around the light just above our small baby's bed. Rachel could imagine just one of those little creatures crawling up Philip's nose and snuffing out his breath. Out of desperation Rachel summoned a young hotel worker to get rid of these creatures. He reluctantly killed one and then took Rachel to the door. He pointed to the small light just outside the door where what seemed like hundreds of lizards feasted on mosquitoes. Since anything is better than mosquitoes, we learned to live with these lizards for all of our years in Asia and surprisingly became quite fond of them.

Since our visas for Vietnam apparently would not arrive soon, I immediately became interim pastor of the Kowloon Baptist Church (English language). Many missionaries of various mission groups attended the evening services held in the Baptist Pooi Ching Middle School auditorium in Kowloon near our hotel. As a young, 30-year-old missionary fresh on the mission field, I was intimidated to preach to missionaries whose names were legendary among the great China missionary corps. As I stood in the pulpit that first day looking over such an illustrious congregation, I wondered what someone like me, so young and inexperienced, could say to such great servants of God. I realized that all I could do would be to study the Word of God, be filled with our Lord's presence, and share what He gave me to share. I could offer no more than that.

One by one these great missionaries very kindly and patiently shared with me their need for the simple presentation of God's Word and to have an opportunity to worship and be inspired in order to carry out the challenges which they met from day to day as they served among the Chinese people. With that encouragement, I settled in for a long wait and a fruitful ministry. Rachel and I taught English in the middle school. I taught Greek in the Baptist seminary. I taught Bible classes in English at night in homes. I found this to be one of the best ways to learn who people are, how they think, and to learn about their culture. They constantly tried to express themselves in English. In so doing they shared matters that were important to them.

One night as I was teaching English using the Ten Commandments as a text, I asked the question, "Is stealing ever right?" The class members immediately held a discussion which I did not understand. Then one student responded in English with the consensus answer. "It depends on who you are stealing from," he said. "If you take from a wealthy person, you are taking from his plenty. If you take from a poor person, you should be punished severely, because he will have so little left." This was not exactly the answer I wanted, but it pointed up an important fact. I learned that many non-Christian Asians have trouble accepting absolute statements. They prefer not to have to judge something as completely black or white. They prefer, instead, to have general statements which leave room to assess the situation and then make a judgment accordingly.

One night I was asking each student what he or she did for a living. One young student responded, "I make antiques." I was a bit surprised at this and asked further, "How can you make antiques?" He replied, "I take new things and make them look old. People like to buy old things!"

During this first Bible class on the mission field, I had the privilege of leading two young men to know Jesus Christ as Lord and Savior. I thoroughly enjoyed seeing them struggle with their lives and the problems of faith and then make those eternal decisions to follow Christ. What could have been many wasted months of simply sitting and waiting idly for something to happen—our visas—became a veritable school of mission work. Those months were filled with wonderful experiences of learning, walking with the Lord, and trusting Him for life and ministry.

In August, official word arrived from the Vietnamese Embassy that our visas had been denied. Under no circumstances could we receive permission to enter Vietnam. We were crushed. After all these months, certain of God's call, we were faced with defeat. After much prayer we decided not to accept this negative answer. We immediately applied again. The weeks passed; no answer arrived. Finally in early October Rachel said, "October 17 is my birthday. My name will be on prayer calendars for missionaries for the very first time. People everywhere will be praying for us on that day. God is going to hear and work a wonderful miracle for us!"

The morning of October 17 arrived. We spent the day in prayer. About 2 in the afternoon we received a call from the Vietnamese Embassy. The embassy said that it had just received a cable from Saigon addressed to us. Embassy personnel asked, "Would you like us to read it to you on the phone, or would you prefer to come to the Embassy and pick it up?" With great anticipation we said, "Read it." It read something like this: "Your request for permission to enter Vietnam has been granted. You may proceed at your convenience within the next 30 days." We had no doubt that the prayers of thousands of people for us that day had been answered within the timing and perfect will of God. As it turned out, missionaries Herman Hayes and Lewis Myers, who resided in Saigon, had been trying every possible way to get our visa request into a position to be considered. Our application had been lying for months in the drawer of a government functionary without being given any opportunity for consideration. By his own admission he said that he was afraid that granting visas to evangelical missionaries would embarrass the government's Roman Catholic President. The personal intervention of our American ambassador, Frederick Nolting, was required to get our visa reconsidered and granted by the Vietnamese government. This act in itself was miraculous and at least partially the result of the tremendous prayer network in action on October 17, 1962.

One of the first things we thought when we heard this news was that after all of these months, we'd be willing to live in anything, anywhere, when we got to Vietnam. Three children 3 years old and under in one stateroom two decks down for three weeks, followed by five months in one room on the third floor of a small, Chinese hotel prepared us well for any place the Lord would give us to live!

Thus we began our missionary career in Vietnam with a miracle from God. This experience was to become a watershed for us as we struggled through uncertain times and almost insurmountable difficulties. Like Israel of old, in uncertain times we often had to go back and recall that miraculous experience and draw fresh sustenance from it. To begin one's ministry with that kind of assurance from God is an indescribable blessing. No doubt because of all those people across the nation who were praying for us on that birthday, we were greatly encouraged that indeed God does answer the prayers of the faithful and can remove every barrier and hindrance to the progress of God's work around the world.

As the years went by, life in the midst of the Vietnam situation could attest only to the miraculous and continuous presence of our Lord in the lives of his people. This was one of those experiences that taught us that no matter how dark the situation seems, God always has something He is teaching us. Sometimes God's timing is highly different from ours. We get impatient and frustrated. Sometimes God's will is different from our will. We cannot understand why we cannot do what we feel called to do by that very will of God. Yet, He has a way of responding when His timing is right and when He is ready for us to fulfill that calling in accordance with His will.

CHAPTER 2

Discussion Questions

Chapter 2 presents a dilemma: Do you continue with your perceived "call of God" even though serious barriers seem to block the
way, or, do you simply recognize that a world of options is available, so you seek an option which presents fewer barriers?

In view of what you just read in Chapter 2, use the following
questions as an opportunity to discuss your own spiritual pilgrimage
as a follower of Jesus.

Questions for discussion:

1. What makes a follower of Jesus continue to pursue what
appears to be a "call" of God to walk a certain path when every
experience along the way seems to have a chilling effect on that call
and even at times to negate the call?

2. When you hear of a miraculous answer to the prayers of
God's people, what does that do to your own commitment to prayer
and dependence on prayer?

3. Do times of trial, discomfort, inconvenience, and hindrance
ever seem to you to be "a school of spiritual growth" that prepare
you for future service for the Lord? How does it prepare you?

Chapter 3

The Night I Became a Missionary

The clock showed 5 in the morning. I stood looking over our living room and into the kitchen. The back door was standing open. The pit of my stomach had a deep, sinking feeling in it. Someone had just stolen almost everything that we owned! The toys, including new bicycles, that the children had just received for Christmas all were gone. My stereo and speakers were gone. In the kitchen, food was taken, along with numerous appliances and utensils.

My family was living about 12 kilometers north of Saigon in a little village called Thu Duc. Our mission had asked me to establish the Vietnam Baptist Theological Seminary there. I was serving as president. New Year's Eve had seen our family playing games and staying up late to welcome the New Year. We all went to bed shortly after midnight. For some reason, at around 5 in the morning, I awoke and was conscious of a strange sense of uneasiness. I decided to check around the house to see if anything was wrong. The scene that greeted me in the living room of our home told me why. I then realized that we had been robbed.

I quickly ran outside to see if anyone might still be around. The streets were deserted. First I felt a deep sense of disappointment and regret. Then anger began to take over. I seethed for days.

Two weeks later, several seminary students awakened me early in the morning. They said, "Pastor, get here quick. Someone has broken into the seminary and stolen almost everything we have." When I arrived at the seminary, I saw that someone had stolen bags of rice, kitchen appliances, bowls, chopsticks, and about everything else they could possibly carry off. They broke into my office and took all of our new office equipment.

With this second robbery I was plunged into a myriad of feelings. I literally seethed with anger. Again and again I said to myself,

"I have traveled 12,000 miles from home to Vietnam to help people and minister to them. What do I get for it? They steal me blind!"

We began a search to find out if any of the students was involved, but nothing turned up. We went to the police station in the nearby village. The police were no help at all. I began to keep a watch at night to see if I could see anything unusual happening. Three nights after the seminary was robbed, I saw a strange sight. Around 1 a.m. a police Jeep stopped about 100 yards up the road from our house. Two police officers got out carrying what looked to be large, empty sacks. I continued to watch. About 30 minutes later the police Jeep blinked its lights twice. Two men stepped out of the shadows on the side of the road and walked to the police Jeep. They had two sacks filled with something. The two sacks were thrown into the Jeep. The Jeep left without turning on any headlights. The next morning I heard that another house had been robbed.

I went to the police station and asked to see the director of the police. He welcomed me into his office and asked what he could do for me. I told him what I had seen and that I suspected that these were the people who had just broken into my home and the seminary and had stolen all of our possessions. I believed that he surely would want to know this since the ones doing this were police officers. He was polite and said that he would look into it.

Two nights later a young police officer dressed in civilian clothes visited our house. He seemed nervous. He said that he had known of my family and me for a long time. He was familiar with Christianity but was not a Christian yet. He said that he greatly respected my family and the seminary students. He regretted that we had been robbed. Then he said, "I am here on my own volition to help you to understand something very important. This village doesn't have much police protection out here. I advise you not to investigate this robbery any more. The story you told our police director greatly disturbs all of us. If you continue your investigation, something bad will happen to you. I want to warn you and try to prevent that from happening. No one knows that I have visited here tonight, but I assure you that I know what I am talking about. Please leave it alone. Go on with your work." With that he left our house. I did not pursue the matter any further, but it simply increased the anger and helplessness I felt and added a high level of frustration. I had absolutely nowhere I could turn for help.

A few days later I got in my van to go into the city. When I turned the key, nothing happened. I checked the various systems and determined that I probably had a dead battery. When I went to take the battery out, I discovered that the battery was not dead. It was gone! Someone had stolen the battery right out of my car.

Weeks later, one of the Protestant chaplains in the U.S. Air Force at the large military base in Cam Ranh Bay called and asked if I would be willing to help the Protestant men of the Air Force Chapel get Vietnamese government permission to set up an orphanage. They wanted to find a way to help the many children whose parents had been killed in the war. They needed someone to be a liaison with the Vietnamese government to see what needed to be done to gain permission to open the orphanage. I agreed to help.

I went to the appropriate ministry of government and asked what needed to be done to get permission to open an orphanage. The young woman gave me a stack of forms to fill out. The stack was at least three inches high. I filled out the forms in duplicate and returned them to the ministry. She looked through them and said, "You should have filled them out in triplicate." With that she gave me additional forms. I took them home and filled them out in triplicate. Returning them to the ministry, I waited while she looked through them. She then said, "You are short one form." I asked her for the form, took the entire file home, filled out that one form in triplicate, and took it all back. By now my attitude was less than honorable! The young woman gave me a receipt and suggested that I wait for her to contact me.

Six weeks later a person in the military called and asked about the progress of the application. I went to the ministry and inquired. A young woman went to look for the file. After almost an hour she returned to the counter and said, "What application is this? What are you asking to do?" I showed her my receipt for the file. She took it and about one hour later returned to say, "I am sorry. I can't locate your file. I think we have lost it."

I was furious. I never had seen such inefficiency. I asked for the forms again, took them home, filled them all out in triplicate, returned them to the ministry, and asked for a receipt. I tried my best to smile and be polite. Inside I was filled with anger. Somehow this was added to the recent events of stealing and robbery and simply intensified a growing sense of frustration, helplessness, and anger.

A few days later, on Saturday afternoon, I was in Saigon for the day. When I got into my Volkswagen van to return home, it would not start. No matter what I did, I could not fix it. Because frequent "fire fights" occurred on the road between Thu Duc and Saigon, I needed to be home by sunset. I asked several taxis before I could find one willing to take me the 12 kilometers home. No one wanted to drive on that road in the late afternoon. I boarded the taxi; we began the trip weaving in and out through the maze of pedestrians, bicycles, trucks, army Jeeps, horses and wagons, motorcycles, ox carts, and every other imaginable vehicle. The taxi driver asked politely, "You have been in Vietnam a long time, haven't you?"

I replied, "Yes, for many years."

He then asked, "Then you must like the Vietnamese people?"

At that point in my life, answering this question was difficult, given all that had happened recently. My house was broken into. My car battery was stolen. The seminary was robbed. Even the effort to help war babies by starting an orphanage had become a nightmare. I thought about the fact that I am a Christian, a missionary, a pastor, and a seminary president. I replied in a manner appropriate to my titles if not a bit hypocritically, "Oh yes. I love the Vietnamese people!"

In the midst of all the traffic, he turned his face toward me, looked straight into my eyes, and asked, "What do you love about us?" What a horrible time to ask me a question like that! I wanted to say to him, "Don't push it, brother! I don't want to talk about it!" He could have asked a million questions without asking that one! Given all that had happened over previous weeks, this was not a good time. I braced myself and tried my best to answer his question. Whatever I said in reply could not have been significant. The taxi drove into my yard. I paid him the exorbitant fare that he exacted of me and went into the house dejected. Rachel had dinner on the table. I tried to eat, but I had a huge lump in my throat from the emotions caused by the question he had asked. I was deeply concerned about my state of mind and attitude. My love for the Vietnamese people was gone!

I always have believed that if you could take the Christian faith, put it in a pot on a stove, and boil away all of the excess until all you have left is its purest essence, that would be love—God's kind of love. That purest essence of the Christian faith when everything else is stripped away is God's unconditional love. I realized that I no longer possessed that kind of love within me. I wondered if it had ever really been there. At any rate, it was gone now. I had allowed the circumstances of life to destroy it.

I went to bed but could not sleep. After tossing and turning for hours, I went into our living room, knelt down by the couch, and began to pour my heart out to the Lord. I confessed my lack of love for the very people among whom I lived in order to be God's servant. I confessed my disappointment because I had allowed the negative events of life to take away my love for the people. During my prayer I saw that I had a big decision to make. I had failed as a missionary. I had failed as a true servant of the Lord. How could I stay on the mission field if I did not have the very essence of the Christian faith that I was offering to others? I decided that the best thing was for me to begin the process of packing up our few remaining belongings that very morning. I was through as a missionary. No matter how much I tried to go back to bed, the Lord would not let me go. I continued in prayer all night.

Sometime in the wee hours of the morning, God spoke to me. I have noticed that sometimes only when our backs are completely against the wall and our strength is completely gone, that this is when God steps in and intervenes. I have no doubt that God Himself intervened in my life in those moments of total defeat. His words seemed to well up in my heart. They penetrated my consciousness with unmistakable and clear thought. It was a feeling of absolute oneness and intimacy.

God said to me, "My son, you are not in Vietnam because you love the Vietnamese people. You are here because I love them. I want to love them through you."

God loved the Vietnamese people before I was ever born. God loves all of the peoples of the world even from the foundation of the world. Throughout history God has been in the process of communicating that love. He communicated His love by becoming flesh and blood in Jesus Christ. In Christ we have become the vehicles by which God now wants to communicate His love. We often confuse our human love with His eternal love. Human love is so fragile. One word can destroy human love. One gesture or facial expression can take away our human love. But God's love is eternal. Nothing can separate us from God's love. God's love knows no condition. His love is freely given.

When I received my divine call to go to Vietnam, I did not know one Vietnamese person. I did not know one word in the Vietnamese language. I knew nothing of the people of Vietnam, their customs, and their culture. I only knew that God was calling me there. How could I love them when I did not even know them? Why did God choose Rachel and me to go there to those people? Now I know that God had something of ultimate importance that He wanted to communicate to them through our lives. I had given my life to the Lord to be used by Him. Then the divine call occurred. For a long time in Vietnam my love for the people seemed to grow. My interest and absorption into the life of the people and their culture was exciting. I was excited to learn their language. I enjoyed their food. My commitment to them was unquestionable. Humanly speaking, I really loved them. But human love is too fragile to weather the tests and trials of cross-cultural living. I have no doubt that God Himself called me and engendered in me the interest and love for the Vietnamese people. Why? Because He needed someone to go to them and embody His great love for them and to communicate His desire that they become saved. The problem was that I saw that call as my call more than His call to me. I saw that love as my love, not His love. I was trying to fulfill that calling in my power, not His power.

Vietnam, like most cultures around the world, is a non-Christian culture. Therefore, the people conduct themselves by a value system that is not informed by Christian teachings and God's love. They were a culture which was being torn apart by war. Every day of their lives carried a threat to their continued existence. The Vietnamese people had to learn to survive. To survive in that hostile society, they had to become tough. They had to find every way possible to provide the necessities of life. The one thing that they had no chance of finding was the peace and contentment derived from experiencing God's unconditional love. Thus the behavior that so destroyed my human love was natural for them because they never have known anything else.

I had gone to Vietnam as a Christian and a missionary, because the Vietnamese people were lost without Christ. They deserved the opportunity to know Jesus and to be saved. I had no right to expect them to live their lives and conduct themselves as Christians. When they robbed me, or acted as though they had little care or concern for their own people, I had no right to become angry and condemn them. This kind of behavior was the very reason God placed me in their midst to show them a better way and a more eternal way. Why would I cease to be a Christian simply because people acted less than Christian? Why should I cease my missionary calling simply because the people acted like people who do not know Jesus? My very purpose in life was to help them know Christ and have a new life in Him!

What I did not realize was that my human love was so fragile and that my human strength was so weak that it could not take the stress of that environment. I simply could not do it in my own power and love. I would have to be emptied of myself, my own power, my own love or lack of it, and then filled to overflowing with His power, His eternal love, and the very presence of Jesus Himself.

There, in the early hours of that morning, I realized in a fresh new way what the apostle Paul was saying in his letter to the Galatian Christians. He said, "I have been crucified with Christ; and it is no longer I who live, but Christ lives in me; and the life which

I now live in the flesh I live by faith in the Son of God, who loved me, and delivered Himself up for me" (Gal. 2:20).

Clearly what I had to do was to place myself on the altar and die so that He could live through me. My only choice was to surrender my life totally to the Lord and allow Him to empty me completely and re-fill me with His presence. I would have to become one with Him in a way that I never had experienced before. My love, or lack of it, would have to give way to His eternal, unconditional love. My strength would have to become His strength.

All my Christian life I had talked about the Christian incarnating the gospel even as God became incarnate in Christ. Jesus' last words, as recorded in the New Testament before He ascended into heaven after his resurrection, were to His disciples, "As the Father has sent me, I also send you" (John 20:21). Now this commission had to reach a new level of reality in my life. It was a miraculous time of experiencing the ministry of the Lord in my life—remolding and remaking me into a new person and a new instrument in God's hands.

The following morning I was walking through a market area. I had walked through there many times before. A woman with leprosy always sat at the entrance to the market. She had pads of ragged material wrapped around her arms, knees, and feet to pull herself along the ground into the market entryway, where she would sit and beg all day. She sat on a bamboo mat day after day with a small bowl in front of her and hoped that someone would drop in a coin. Leprosy almost had completed its work of deforming her body. A gaping hole now was where her nose used to be. Huge holes were on each side of her head where her ears had been. One tooth protruded at an angle from her mouth. Her fingers and toes were completely gone. Her face was so deformed, it was hardly recognizable as a face. Up to now, always when I walked by her, I turned my face away to keep from looking at her.

On this morning I looked at her as though I was seeing her through Jesus' eyes. I never had experienced such feelings of compassion for anyone. I realized that probably no person in the world loved this woman in this condition. Surely no one ever touched her, or talked with her, or showed any kind of love for her. I could not resist sitting down on the edge of her mat. I began to talk to her. I told her how much God loves her. I told her that this body deteriorates and rots away, but someday it can be replaced with a heavenly body when we enter the presence of God in eternity. I talked to her about Jesus and how she can find forgiveness, hope, and eternal salvation in Him. I searched her face to see if she had some faint flicker of recognition of what I was saying. The disease had so ravaged her body that most likely the muscles in her face could not allow a response. Every morning I stopped by to see her. Sometimes I would place my hand on her shoulder or touch her gnarled nub where her fingers once were. I always looked for some response. Some weeks later, as I talked to her one morning, I was almost sure that I saw a tear in her eye.

Much later I began to realize that this was a picture of how God relates to us. We are sinners—far from what God created us to be. Sin ravages our life and utterly distorts the image of God in us. God keeps approaching us in His great eternal love. Even though our behavior reflects no response to that love, He never gives up or ceases to love us. No doubt our behavior and attitudes often are so abhorrent that normal bounds of human reasoning would expect Him to turn His face away from us. But, His love is eternal and keeps reaching out regardless of our sin. God does not want any one to perish without knowing His eternal love which He has given to us in Christ Jesus.

I often have thought how loving an old leper woman, so physically deformed as she, is easier than is loving someone who is spiritually or emotionally unlovely. Often we have those in the same household, or in the same church, or in the same class or workplace, who are so very hard to love. They hurt us. They reject us. Perhaps they consciously or unconsciously do things that threaten our good name or our sense of well being. I, myself, was living in the midst of an entire society that in many ways was very much like this. We have every reason to turn away from them. Our fragile, human love cannot possibly survive. However, a love transcends all of that. That love is God's love. His love is eternal. It requires no response but the response of genuine love returned. It demands no reward. It is love purely for the sake of love. The only way change can occur in them or us is when we so fall in love with our Lord and focus on Him and become one with Him that He is able to love through us when we no longer can. He takes our hands, our feet, our voice, our gifts, and our talents, and fills them with His ministering presence.

We devise all kinds of strategies and clever plans to try to communicate and get people to respond to the reality of Jesus. Churches develop great goals, objectives, and action plans to get more people into the church. Missionaries develop intricate strategies to accomplish the task of bringing all the peoples of the world to a saving faith in Jesus. The truth is, no strategies, goals, objectives, and action plans are worth the paper on which they are written unless those who would carry them out are empowered by the eternal love and compassion of Christ and filled with His presence. We first of all must "be" and only then can we "do" with any semblance of God's divine power.

CHAPTER 3

Discussion Questions

Chapter 3 presents a dilemma: When love fails because of negative human experiences, does one simply accept that love has not been sufficient and move on, or, does one continue in the situation until God reveals another way?

Use the following questions to discuss your own spiritual pilgrimage as a follower of Jesus.

1. Should we carry the gospel only to those people who treat us kindly and fairly? Or should we carry the Good News of salvation to all the people whether or not they act kindly and fairly towards us?

2. In view of what you have read in this chapter, what are some of the differences in human love versus divine love?

3. How does a person replace "human love" with "God's love"?

4. Should the author of this chapter have continued to pursue those who were stealing from the village in spite of the police officer's warning? Wouldn't the courageous thing have been to try to change the culture and bring an end to the lawlessness in the village? What would you have done?

Chapter 4

Secret Place of the Most High

Some scenes from one's past never fade or lose their intensity as long as life lasts. Such was the scene that stretched out before me on a fateful Sunday afternoon in 1965. The sounds, the smells, and the resultant wrenching that began slowly in the pit of my stomach and threaded its way with growing intensity into my throat always will be there wherever I go, whatever I do.

The scene on the road to My Tho was beyond belief. Five cars now were gutted shells, burned beyond recognition. Nineteen bodies lay twisted grotesquely along the side of the road. Some still smoldered from the intense heat. Some had gaping holes here and there. The air reeked of gunsmoke still floating heavily across the rice fields and the roadway.

Less than two hours before, I had been the second car in a line of cars stopped at a roadblock in this very place. Now, miraculously alive and well, I stood surveying the spot where I recently had been stopped. I looked at those who had just been wiped violently from the face of the earth.

All of this had begun a month earlier. A letter arrived from My Tho, a delta city and a village some 150 kilometers south of Saigon on a tributary of the Mekong River. I recognized the name on the letter as that of a young woman whom I had led to a saving knowledge of Jesus Christ during an Intervarsity Christian Fellowship student retreat two years before. I was a frequent speaker for these Saigon University student retreats and had seen dozens of students trust Christ. This young woman stood out in my memory because of her rapid growth in the faith and her deep commitment to the Lord. In September, on graduating from college, the government had sent her to teach in a rather large, rural middle school near the village of My Tho. It was an unusually large school for such a small community. Very few Christian students were there; no Christians were on the faculty when she arrived.

Her letter invited me to visit her school for an afternoon rally on December 26 and to share with the students and faculty the real meaning of Christmas. She told in detail of the intense interest among her students. She was witnessing to them but had little help from other sources. She felt very isolated and needed someone to help support her Christian testimony. Her plea was quite emotional and had a sense of urgency about it.

She had invited me on two previous occasions, but I had been unable to go and for good reason. The road to this village often was insecure, with communist troops frequently causing unrest and trouble in the entire area. As missionaries in Vietnam we had agreed that we had enough work to do in the cities without going out into the insecure and dangerous countryside unless we absolutely had to do so. If we had already begun a great deal of our work in the countryside, as had the Christian and Missionary Alliance Mission through its long history, we then would, of necessity, be involved in outlying areas. However, our strategy from the beginning called primarily for the winning of the cities to Christ. Thus, I could not just get in my car and make my way to this rural government school.

As the days went by I simply could not get this invitation out of my mind. Time and again I attempted to write a polite decline. Every time I prayed I could see hundreds of Vietnamese students seated before me, waiting for the good news of Jesus Christ. When I closed my eyes to sleep, I could see the bright, young, hopeful faces lifted intently to hear God's Word taught to them. When I reasoned with myself, I would repeat over and over that Christmas is an unusual time of openness to the story of God's sending Jesus Christ to earth to reveal Himself to all humankind, even to these rural school children. How could I decline such an invitation? This was my very reason for being a missionary in Vietnam.

I began to pray earnestly about this matter. Gradually an unmistakable and inexplicable peace of mind and heart occurred in me about going. I talked at length with Rachel and found that she, too, had this peace. I then notified the young Christian teacher that I was preparing to arrive but would want to be able to cancel if security on the road should become a problem. Her reply was enthusiastic. She already had begun preparation. More than 500 middle-school and junior-high students would be present along with most of the faculty. I became excited beyond description at the potential of this meeting.

Late on the day of December 25, I called the Vietnamese security office, which has responsibility for the military districts south of Saigon extending to the vicinity of My Tho. They reported that the road was secure. No incidents had been recorded on that road for several weeks. They advised that on my return to Saigon I was to arrive near the city limits by sunset at the latest. Early on the morning of December 26, I called the American military security police. They informed me that they considered the road to be secure during the daylight hours. However, they would advise no unnecessary stops along the road and a return to Saigon by late afternoon. With this last check I believed that all was clear for the trip. Soon after that call I decided to spend my morning quiet time in one of my favorite passages—Psalm 91. Later, this would prove to be the best decision of that entire, fateful day.

Around 8:30 in the morning I said good-bye to Rachel and my children. I knew that I would have to cross two rivers by ferry and a drawbridge, which could delay my arrival by hours depending on the river traffic. The entire trip could take up to five hours. I was hoping to arrive at the ferry landings at the right time to avoid the long wait in line under a very hot sun. In those days no cars in Vietnam had air conditioning. Out on the road in the delta of Vietnam, the temperature on the road could rise well above 100 degrees with high humidity. The rainy season had passed. Although this would be approaching the coolest time of the year, being in the sun still could be unbearable. To wait on the road under those conditions, even with a gentle breeze, was debilitating, to say the least. Too, the threat of some kind of terrorist attack anywhere a crowd of people was gathered existed. An American standing alone in a crowd of Vietnamese people would make a fine target for any terrorist. Many times in past months, as I stood preaching in an open field before hundreds of Vietnamese, this very thought flashed before my mind. A missionary in Vietnam had to learn to live with such thoughts. We never were away from potential tragedy and disaster. I always would allow such thoughts to surface only for a brief moment and then put them aside. I had no room to entertain fear. One could not survive long in Vietnam with fear occupying a prominent part of one's thinking.

My work as director of theological education called for a great deal of flying from city to city to assist and oversee theological education-by-extension centers. This flying was done on the local Vietnamese airline, Air Vietnam. Most of the planes were leased or had been purchased many years before. Many were old DC-3 aircraft, which had been built during the Second World War and made available to Vietnam as a part of American aid.

These two-engine planes often were described as the most dependable planes ever put into the air. No doubt they were, but 25 years of constant use was begging the point! Often in the evening, before I was to fly the next day, I would slip quietly into my children's bedroom after they were asleep. I would stand there and look down at those small, blond heads and feel a terrible heaviness of heart that something might happen tomorrow which would leave them fatherless.

At those times I often was very near to resigning my missionary career and returning to the United States. Then, the next morning the brightness of the dawn would dispel feelings of foreboding. The challenge and excitement of what God could do through me that day would replace the crippling disease of fear, which focuses so much attention on self-paralyzing thought and action. I knew in my heart that nothing is wrong with fear and that every person experiences it. But I knew, too, that if I did not fight fear and overcome it, my missionary career in a place like Vietnam never would be able to continue.

I soon was on the outskirts of Saigon, well past the crowded traffic. As I moved south, the rice paddies stretched to the horizon as far as the eye could see. The landscape was broken only by an occasional clump of palm trees marking the end of one series of paddies and the beginning of another. Here and there a farmhouse rose as though emerging right up out of a rice paddy. The rainy season over, no more clouds would be in the sky for the next five months until May. The constant sun had put final touches on the rice crop in early December. Farmers almost had completed their harvest. The further south I went, the more brown and bare were the paddy lands—the earth baked under a scorching sun. I felt a little disappointed, because few scenes are more beautiful than golden fields of rice, ready for harvest, waving in a gentle breeze. Each moment they bring a slightly different hue of brown, orange, and yellow.

Before harvest, the farmer breaks the paddy dike and allows the water to drain out. Then the entire family enters the field to cut the rice by hand. Centuries of use had built up a delicate layer of clay underneath the paddy; thus forming something of a bowl that would hold water during the critical planting and growing stage. To bring in heavy cultivating and harvest equipment on this fragile paddy easily would crush the protective under-layer, destroying the capability of holding water. In the early 1950s the Chinese had attempted mechanized farming of huge tracts of paddy land. Those lands in China took many years to recover.

As I sped along, I was glad to be out of the crowded city with its polluted air. I breathed in deeply the fresh, clean country air and felt a new sense of freedom. Having grown up in the fresh, country air of a little town in North Carolina, I had not easily adjusted to life in a teeming city of more than three million people.

The traffic just ahead was stopped at the crossroads of a little village. A Vietnamese army convoy was approaching. Whatever the situation, the army always had the right of way over civilian traffic. As soon as I pulled off the road to stop, my car was besieged by little boys, girls, old men, and women selling every imaginable kind of merchandise—mostly fresh fruit. The children sold little plastic bags filled with sugar cane cut into round, wafer-like pieces. Lining both sides of the road were stands of fresh pineapple. This area of the country is known for its sweet, delicious pineapple. Wounded veterans, beggars, and lepers seeing an American face literally besieged my car with hands outstretched for whatever I might give.

The press of the people around my car was beginning to be beyond endurance. I was caught in a dilemma. If I raised the windows, the car immediately would become an unbearable furnace. If I left my windows open, I could not avoid the hands reaching in with urgent insistence. This was not the first time I had been convicted of my desire to shut out people who are in need. Never once in all of my years in Vietnam did I become accustomed to not being able to minister to the hordes of people who cried out for help. Experience had taught me, however, that if you help one or two, then all of the others become angry if you cannot help them, too. Riots have been started by well-meaning people trying to give aid to a few out of the many!

Gratefully the traffic began to move forward. Once again I was on my way. I could not help but think of Jesus besieged on the road time and again by the lame, the infirm, the demon-possessed, the blind, and the lepers. They all wanted to be near Jesus—to touch him. But I believed that they were not after Jesus' money or his abundant possessions. I doubt that they could have recognized him as a man of wealth. He was known as the One who had the power to heal them. His disciples often tried to protect him, but to no avail. Whether it was blind Bartimaeus or the woman with a troublesome sickness, Jesus seemed to be able to see each one and minister to them all. I often felt that I could identify with the fatigue that Jesus must have felt trying to deal with the press of the multitude. So often as a missionary I have longed to change the shape of my eyes and the color of my skin and hair. If only I could look like my Vietnamese brothers and sisters, perhaps they would expect something from me other than money or material things. Perhaps they would expect spiritual power and healing from me. Alas, as an American, I must bear the expectations that arise because of it. On some occasions I would step from my car, pass out tracts for them to read, and preach a sermon. On this rather insecure road in the middle of war, I did not dare to do that. The one comforting thing about my being an American was that anywhere I went, I could draw a crowd of people simply by lifting my voice in Vietnamese. My very presence as a Vietnamese-speaking foreigner made them curious. This would open the way for a marvelous witness to Christ. But no roadside sermon would happen that day.

My arrival at each of the ferry landings was just right. My arrival at the drawbridge, just as the traffic began to move across, gave much comfort. This seemed to be another confirmation of God's call and leadership regarding this particular trip. Every aspect of the trip was working smoothly.

I was scarcely four kilometers from the village where the school was located. Knowing that I would be quite early, I had slowed my car a bit and simply enjoyed watching the beautiful landscape of the countryside. As I neared the MeKong River basin, I saw larger trees. The occasional underbrush along the road was much thicker. The land was not as flat as before. The road was not nearly as straight.

Then, as I rounded a curve, I was horrified to see a roadblock less than 300 yards ahead. Dirt was piled half as high as my Volkswagen van and extended all the way across the road. One car already had stopped. I was the second. I knew immediately the significance of this roadblock.

The Viet Cong would pile dirt completely across the road to stop all traffic. At the proper time, soldiers would force everyone out of their cars at gunpoint. They would extol the virtues of communism and contrast this with the corruption of the Vietnamese government and the American "imperialists." After taking watches, rings, money, and other valuables, they would open the roadblock and allow traffic to resume.

Just weeks before this, a Philippine missionary and his baby had been shot to death at such a roadblock in central Vietnam. This death was entirely without provocation. A soldier simply lowered his rifle and fired the fatal shots at the only foreigner in the group. The bullets went through the baby and into the missionary. Both died immediately.

With these thoughts in mind I began applying my brakes to stop. I was so terrified at what might happen that my foot trembled almost uncontrollably. I could not keep it on the brake pedal. I finally stopped some five feet behind the lone car in front of me. Two Vietnamese men and a child were in the front seat of that car.

38

Seconds seemed to pass as slowly as minutes. Thoughts flashed through my mind in rapid succession. My first thoughts were self-blame: *You are stupid! You should have known better than to be out here! You knew it could be fraught with danger. Can you ever learn not to play the hero and get yourself in trouble?* My thoughts turned to my family. Never had I felt so much love and longing for Rachel. My children's faces all were before me at that moment. My heart nearly broke with a yearning to be back with them.

Fear seized me. I trembled all over. I looked off the road to the right and saw low, wild bushes and palmetto ground cover. I could barely make out the large number of camouflaged communist troops scattered through the field well-hidden under the brush. Fear again seized me. My heart beat as it never had beat before. I was an American, which automatically increased the danger for me many-fold. I could not think clearly. Thoughts were flooding my mind. I had no means of escape.

I was the second car in line, but by now, several cars had stopped behind me. On the other side of the roadblock were at least a dozen cars. At the rate cars were stopping, in only a matter of moments the troops would reveal themselves to begin their method-ical search of every individual and vehicle. Panic again surged through my mind and body. Then, the 91st Psalm sprang to mind. I felt as though I had memorized it. Actually, I never had even tried to commit that psalm to memory, though I occasionally had read it and meditated on it. Now the words were in my mind as clear as a bell. "He who dwells in the shelter of the Most High will abide in the shadow of the Almighty. I will say to the Lord, 'My refuge and my fortress, My God, in whom I trust!' For it is He who delivers you from the snare of the trapper, and from the deadly pestilence. He will cover you with His pinions, and under His wings you may seek refuge . . .. You will not be afraid . . .. " (Ps. 91:1-5).

That morning during my quiet time I had thought of the beauty of this psalm. I remember reading with little notice the portion which lists all of the things that the person to whom the psalm was written would not be afraid of, such as the "pestilence that comes by night, the arrows by day." That portion had not been very meaningful to me. Now, the words "You shall not be afraid . . ." literally reverberated through my whole being.

"But God, I am not just afraid right now. I am absolutely terrified beyond control!" I said.

I remember asking God, "What are you saying to me right now through this psalm about fear?" Then, as natural as the dawn itself, I thought about the relationship between fear and trust, which is the heart of what the psalmist was trying to say. The secret place of the Most High is a place of complete and total trust in the Lord. Abiding under the shadow of the Almighty and resting under "His pinions" is like a baby chicken taking perfect rest and security as it trusts its life into its mother's care. I always thought that the opposite of fear is courage, or that the antidote to fear is to be brave. I realized I had been wrong. The antidote to fear is not courage or bravery. It is trust! When complete and total trust is there, fear subsides.

My questions now were of a different kind: *Had I not earnestly prayed for God's will to be done on this trip? Had I not received peace and joy through my prayers and the anticipation of the trip? Had I not checked the security of the roads and taken every precaution? Had I not received confirmation through Rachel? Did I not know beyond a shadow of a doubt that God had led in this decision all the way? Was I not sincerely about my Father's business?* The answer to all of those questions was a resounding "Yes!"

I long have believed in the goodness of God. I believe in His omnipotence and omniscience. I believe that He understands and knows all of our yesterdays, todays, and tomorrows. I believe in the inherent goodness of His perfect will for my life. How could I now, in this moment, forsake everything that I have long held to be true?

Therefore I now knew the source of my fear. I wanted to be in control of my life. I wanted above everything to live. I wanted to continue to be Rachel's husband and my children's father. I was not through with my life. What I needed right at that moment was to submit my entire being into His perfect will.

I no longer asked the Lord to save me. I entered into a state of complete trust that God's will is perfect and good whatever happens to me. Whatever happens by my life or by my death, His perfect, good, and holy will is going to be done. I know that whatever the surface looks like, His will is just and right. At that moment, an absolute trust that God was going to be glorified welled up in me. Over me settled a peace that is beyond description. My entire being seemed to be filled to overflowing with the strong presence of my Lord. I knew, at that moment, that beyond any doubt I was ready to die if need be. The heavens seemed to open; I believed that I actually was in His presence. A marvelous peace settled over me.

I looked to the right. I still saw no movement among the troops hidden there. I looked to the left at a series of rice paddies stretching as far as the eye could see. The roadside gently sloped downward toward the rice paddies at about a 25-degree angle. Between the end of the slope and the nearest paddy was a path the farmers used to drive their water buffalo to and from work in the fields. It was crusted and dry. The hoof marks had left deep holes made when the paddies still were filled with water and the surrounding land was muddy. Deep ruts were evident where occasional carts had been driven along the path to load the harvested rice. I made a decision to risk driving down the embankment to follow this path, if at all possible.

I do not know how long I had sat there. Hours seemed to have passed, though I knew only a few minutes had elapsed. My engine still was running. I was glad I would not have to attract attention by starting it.

I tried not to move my arms perceptibly as I slowly turned the wheels all the way to the left. I then slowly put the car in its lowest gear. Gradually I fed the gas until the car slowly was rolling toward the side of the road. In a moment I was easing down the incline toward the rice paddy and the path alongside it. I expected any moment to hear gunshots ring out and it would then be all over. Instead, I heard only deadly silence. I could see the rather long line of cars stretched out behind me. None of them was moving. I continued down the incline until I reached the path. At that point I picked up speed. I almost shouted with joy as I saw the pathway veer slightly to the left through a thick banana grove, well past the roadblock on the highway above. At times the van seemed as though it would turn over as it rolled in and out of deep ruts and water buffalo tracks. In a moment I was through the banana grove. Only 200 yards ahead I could see the path veering back up onto the highway. Within moments I was on the shoulder on the wrong side of the road facing the lined-up traffic until I found a space through which to proceed. On the highway, I was speeding faster than I ever had driven before. Ahead were the school, the bright young students, and my opportunity to share about Christ.

Just before I arrived at the school I stopped on the side of the road in the shade of a bamboo grove. Suddenly I was so weak that I hardly could lift a hand. I put my head on the steering wheel and thanked God for His miraculous intervention. I then asked the Lord to work one more special miracle in my mind and body. I asked for calmness of mind, so that I could preach the gospel with clarity and unhindered power. I think if I had not had this time of prayer, I could not possibly have walked into that schoolhouse. I never would have had the mind nor energy to preach. The tremendous drain of emotional energy had left me nearly helpless.

Several minutes later, I drove up in front of the school. A welcoming group of students led by the young Christian teacher met me as I got out of my van. Just as we turned to enter the school, a series of heavy muffled explosions shook us all. This was followed by a crescendo of rapid fire from automatic weapons. Thuds, which I recognized to be the sound of hand grenades, echoed across the rice paddies. When I stopped at the roadblock, I had not realized that I was so close to the school. I had no question that this was a battle which was erupting in the vicinity of that roadblock. Soon heavy clouds of thick black smoke towered into the sky. The years in Vietnam had taught me to be sensitive to sights and sounds. I instantly could tell the difference between sounds made by various guns and how close they were. I knew that heavy black smoke meant that one or more vehicles had been set on fire. Gasoline, oil, and tires were burning furiously.

My heart sank as I realized that all of those innocent people still in line at that roadblock were facing the horror from which I had so miraculously escaped. I quickly related to the teachers and students standing around me what had happened.

As I think back on this experience, I now am aware of an interesting phenomenon which occurred. One would think that immediate excitement, concern, anxiety, and questions would be raised by the students and teachers about the possibility that some of their loved ones might have been caught in that roadblock. Instead, I saw only a quiet resignation and saddened faces. Someone quietly suggested that we go ahead into the school for the scheduled program. None of the large number of students already seated in the auditorium rushed out to investigate the shooting. One would think that children all over the world would be filled with curiosity about something such as that. A tremendous battle was going on about four kilometers away, as the crow flies, and these children were seated quietly in their seats waiting for their teachers to arrive.

I suppose when one has lived all of one's life under the sound of gunfire and the threat of death, with all of the accompanying suffering, grief, and disappointment, a fateful resignation sets in as a lifestyle. A few years after this incident I found the same phenomenon happening in my own life. We were living in the little village of Thu Duc, 12 kilometers to the north of Saigon. On the highway were frequent ambushes of army convoys during the night. Our house stood less than 100 yards from the highway. When the first ambush occurred, I jumped out of the bed and watched from the shelter of my backyard. Then, as time went by, more ambushes would occur. We simply would wake up, turn over, and go back to sleep. Unconsciously, we were thinking, "What can we do? We are helpless to change anything or to be of help. The military will have to deal with it."

I often find myself veering to the left and the right of a thin, almost indiscernible line that runs between caring and not caring, wanting to help and not being able to help. Somewhere in between these two is a place where the missionary must walk with a measure of balance.

That day I preached with unusual power. My strength had to spring from God, because I had absolutely no strength or power left in me. Numerous students raised their hands to express an interest in knowing Jesus as Savior. They surged forward to fill out decision cards, which would enable this young teacher to follow up on them. As I left, I felt a strange sadness to leave this brave young woman who was committed to discipling all these young students so hungry for the Christian faith which provided hope in the midst of a life so destitute of hope. I wished so much that I could become several people and place myself in many such places as this to help with these beautiful students.

When the service ended, the sounds of fighting long since had died away. Not much smoke was in the air now. Several students volunteered to accompany me as far as the roadblock. They suggested that I let them out on this side of the site, so that they could walk ahead and determine whether I could proceed safely. Five boys piled into the van with little concern for their own safety. Less than a kilometer from the site they left the van. Within moments they were running back. Their faces were unusually pale.

"It is a terrible scene," they said, "but you can get through safely." I asked what had happened. They replied that a small convoy of Vietnamese government troops had happened along. Seeing the roadblock they had opened fire on the opposing troops in the field. The two sides engaged each other in battle. The cars and people at the roadblock were caught in the crossfire. The people had nowhere to escape. The first two cars on the My Tho side of the roadblock and the first three cars on the other side had burned. Many people were dead. Bodies were all over the road. With this, the boys said good-bye and began walking back to their village. They refused to allow me to take them home. They were concerned for my safety and wanted me on the road as quickly as possible.

That is why I happened to be standing there on that fateful day surveying the unforgettable scene, which never will be erased from my memory. I thought then, even as I realize now, *What if I had not experienced the intervention of the Lord and had allowed fear to paralyze me into inaction? What if the 91st Psalm had not been hidden away in my heart to be called forth at just the right moment as God's unique word to me in an hour of dire need? What if I had been there without Christ and without the peace of God that flowed through my life and heart at just the right moment?* Of course these are unanswerable questions.

I was able to say with all of my heart with the author of the 91st Psalm, that I know beyond any shadow of doubt that "He who dwells in the shelter of the most High will abide in the shadow of the Almighty. I will say to the Lord, 'My refuge and my fortress, my God, in whom I trust!'" (Ps. 91:1-2). With that sense of absolute trust I could say, "I will not be afraid . . . "

In the presence of my Lord, through His Word in my heart and His miraculous peace, I was led to a new and higher plane of faith through one of the most unforgettable days of my life. Never again will the study of theology take on the character of simply an academic discipline for me. All too often reflection and study regarding the reality of God and His activity among humankind had been far too academic. Sadly, such academic understanding can be mistaken for the essence of belief and faith.

I'm not saying that academic discipline is not useful or even good. However, as we walk moment by moment with the Lord in constant companionship with Him, those precious, rare moments of learning occur. What we may have learned academically is confirmed in the crucible of life itself. Such knowledge of God must be able to be experienced in its reality in the critical moments of life, or it is nothing. To live with the Lord when things are light makes real the potential of realizing His presence when things are dark and when finding Him is not easy. The more we value our daily walk with Him when all is going well, the greater the potential of experiencing His fullness when moments of crises come. From the well of rich, historical experiences we are able to draw forth the lessons to be learned from those traumatic times. How wonderful to walk through the deep and frightening waters of life and emerge on the other side with a new understanding of the reality of the presence of God!

CHAPTER 4

Discussion Questions

Chapter 4 contains a significant dilemma: Should one's priority be on safety and security, or should one's priority be to follow a perceived "call" of God regardless of circumstances?

In view of what you have read in chapter 4, use the following questions as an opportunity to discuss your own spiritual pilgrimage as a follower of Jesus.

1. How would you describe the decision to go to this high-risk area to speak to middle-school children and teachers about Jesus? Was it a foolish risk? Was it an informed risk? Was it a risk worth taking regardless of the circumstances? What would you have done?

2. Even in places which are not at war, God sometimes asks us to undertake a task which produces anxiety or fear. What steps would you take to enable you to carry out the task?

3. What is the relationship between "fear", "courage", "bravery", and "absolute trust", when doing the will of God?

4. What would you say is the most valuable lesson the author learned through this experience?

Chapter 5

A Crisis in Perspective

Mrs. Thanh lay motionless on her small hospital cot in the intensive care ward at Binh Dan Hospital. She had been restless—sometimes awake and alert, but most of the time in a fitful sleep. Rachel and I had been with her all day. The scene gradually had turned into a deathwatch. She was critically ill, this young beautiful Vietnamese woman 30 years of age. Now, at 8 o'clock on Saturday night, our thoughts were centered on whether she would live until midnight.

A single bulb hanging from the ceiling lit the room. The walls were bare. A large crack in the old plaster zigzagged its way down one wall. Six patients including Mrs. Thanh were in the room. This room was called the intensive care ward, not because the patients receive more intense care, but because the most intensively sick patients are there. Family members provide almost all their care because of the extreme shortage of medical personnel. The number of family members gathered around their sick loved ones added to the terrible heat in the non-air-conditioned room. At that hour of the evening the temperature outside had cooled to around 90 degrees. With no fans available the temperature inside soared.

Listening to an occasional moan or cough, I reflected on the pitiful medical facilities. What more could one expect in a country which had not known a time of peace during the past 30 years? Now, in 1966, the communist campaign was at its height. War raged in every quarter of the country. The military desperately needed medical personnel. This meant that civilian hospitals like Binh Dan, the largest surgical hospital among the three-million people of Saigon, had few health-care personnel. With 400 beds and about 600 patients on cots and on the floor, health care by trained personnel simply could not be a reality under war conditions.

As I sat there in that small hospital room, my mind went back some three weeks before when Pastor Do Vinh Thanh brought his wife to our home for a visit. Pastor Thanh was one of my choice seminary students. I had helped him to start a new church in a makeshift bamboo shelter on the outskirts of Saigon. Together we had developed that little church from two or three young people who attended the first day to a church of 60 members and a nice building. He now was the proud pastor of that flock. He and I had been through a lot together over the years. I had been present at his wedding ceremony. I was one of the first to see their beautiful son, Tu, at his birth. I had preached the sermon when Pastor Thanh was ordained to the ministry. I often felt myself moving from relationship to relationship with this young pastor. Sometimes I was his seminary teacher. Often he was my teacher about so many things Vietnamese. Sometimes I was his pastor. Often we were like older and younger brothers. Right then I felt like a concerned father.

On that day, he drove into our yard on his motorbike as usual with Mrs. Thanh perched daintily and precariously on the back. Little Tu, now 2 years old, was seated on the front of the bike with Pastor Thanh. I could tell something was wrong. Usually when they visited us, their faces beamed with the joy of the Lord. Today something was different. They entered our house quietly, almost reverently. We knew that Mrs. Thanh had been having health problems. They related to us how they had been to several hospitals and had consulted every medical doctor they could find, but they had no diagnosis and saw no improvement in her health. All hope seemed exhausted. Besides having medical problems Mrs. Thanh was pregnant. They feared for the life of the baby. They turned desperately to Rachel for guidance.

Rachel was the only missionary nurse among our missionaries and had become something of a medical authority for many of the Vietnamese Christians. We decided that Rachel would go with Mrs. Thanh to the Binh Dan Hospital and stay with her until some diagnosis was made. In the course of the visit the doctor proposed that the only way to find out was to do exploratory surgery. Two days later Rachel helped carry Mrs. Thanh into the operating room and then took a seat beside Pastor Thanh just outside the door to the operating theater.

Since no one closed the operating room door, those gathered outside could watch the entire operation. Rachel was stunned to see the surgeon lifting up Mrs. Thanh's intestines through the gaping hole in her abdomen. The surgeon then examined them piece by piece. Within moments the doctor stepped through the door and said to Pastor Thanh, "Mrs. Thanh has a massive malignant tumor, which has completely invaded her abdomen and intestines. We can do nothing." He then added, "By the way, the baby was a boy."

Words cannot possibly describe the tragedy of that moment as this young pastor accepted the reality of the situation. Some time later Mrs. Thanh was taken to the intensive care ward, where she now neared her final moments.

Rachel and I were at her bedside on Saturday night with Pastor Thanh. We waited for the inevitable. All day long we had taken turns wiping the sweat from her fevered brow. This was about all we could do. Application of cold water seemed to cool the fever and ease her delirium. For nearly two hours now Rachel had stood holding under Mrs. Thanh's nose one end of a small rubber hose carrying oxygen from a tank under the bed. This seemed to help Mrs. Thanh to breathe better.

I remember sitting at the end of the bed looking up into Rachel's face as she stood there bone tired. She never left this young woman's side for even a moment. Rachel had trained at one of the finest medical centers in the world—Duke University Medical Center in Durham, NC. She had learned to provide nursing care using the most sophisticated equipment that medical science had to offer. Now she stood in 90-degree heat in a dingy hospital room trying to provide life-giving air to a dying woman through a crudely rigged oxygen tube. The contrast was overwhelming. The truth is that some places in the world, such as the United States, possess so much while most of the world barely survives with the most minimal resources. Why are Americans so privileged to have every possible resource available, yet most of the rest of the world lives and dies at the mercy of life's circumstances? The truth also is that when the time arrives, death has a way of claiming its victims with or without this highly technical medical care. Perhaps having someone like Rachel, with her superb training and loving Christian care, was better than having all the equipment in the world but not having the personal, loving spirit to support in time of crisis. How devastating that so much of this world suffers through life and death without either!

In another corner of the ward, a 6-year-old boy lay on a cot. For hours he had been gasping for breath. Occasionally the silence was broken by his weak cry, "*Nouc, nouc*" (water, water). His gasps for air became more regular with each passing hour until the agonizing moment of his death. Rachel said urgently, "He needs a tracheotomy" (a hole cut in his throat to allow him to breathe). I ran out of the room frantically looking for a medical doctor. Not a single medical doctor was present in the hospital. The boy died.

I left the room deeply troubled by all of the thoughts flooding my being. Just outside the door was a small courtyard. I walked out into the darkness and wandered aimlessly. Tears coursed down my cheeks as I thought over and over again, "It's not fair! It's not fair! Why are so many people in this world called on to suffer endlessly with so little help? We are all human beings with the same physical makeup, the same emotions, the same precious relationships, yet some people in this world are so desperately without hope!"

I found a small, cement bench on the edge of the courtyard. A light was shining onto the bench through the louver at the top of a door. I sat down and took out of my pocket a small New Testament with the psalms in the back. I began to turn from verse to verse as though searching desperately for an answer to my struggling heart. I was drawn to the 24th Psalm and began reading as though I never had seen it before.

"The earth is the Lord's and all it contains. The world and those dwell in it. For He has founded it upon the seas, and established it upon the rivers. And who may ascend into the hill of the Lord? who may stand in His holy place? He who has clean hands and a pure heart."

At that point I stopped. The word "hands" caused me to look down at my own hands. I found myself saying intensely, "Would to God that I could have taken these hands and skillfully cut the tracheotomy in that little boy's throat, letting the clear, fresh air surge into his stifled lungs. Would to God that I could take these hands and perform all those necessary skills which would bring life and ease suffering in countless scores of helpless, hopeless people in this war-ravaged country! Oh God, what does it really mean to have 'clean hands'"?

I read that psalm again and again. As I read, I realized that a great truth was here. I always had thought that when the psalmist referred to "clean hands and a pure heart", he was using a typical Hebrew parallelism. That is, he simply was repeating the same idea in a different way. Now, I began to believe that something significantly different was here. The idea of a "pure heart" is very clear. It has to do with forgiveness and cleansing. First John 1:7 says " . . . and the blood of Jesus His Son cleanses us from all sin." David cried out in Psalm 51:10 "Create in me a clean heart, O God, and renew a steadfast spirit within me." This occurs through the blood of Jesus Christ by which our sins are forgiven and our heart is made pure. But what does it mean to have "clean hands?"

Hands symbolize the activity of life. They say something about what we do with our life. They represent work, play, and the commitment of life. What makes them clean? As I sat reflecting on this, I realized that hands are clean when we give them back to the One who created them for His use. They are clean when they are committed to His purpose for which He made them. Hands have a way of fulfilling the desire of the one who controls them.

• I can take these hands and strike with a single blow.
• I can take these same hands and at the right moment touch a troubled soul and bring immeasurable comfort.
• I can take these hands and make something unbelievably dirty.
• I can take these same hands and bring cleansing and refreshing beauty.
• I can take these hands and rend something into a multitude of disconnected, meaningless pieces.

• I can take these same hands and with a myriad of pieces build something with meaning, beauty, and usefulness.

• I can take these hands and in the brevity of a moment bring death where once was life.

• I can take these same hands and in numerous ways enhance life, instead of death.

• Everything depends on who controls the hands and what life's purpose is deemed to be.

I slipped to my knees beside that cement bench in the darkness of the hospital courtyard and prayed, "Oh, God, how often I have used these hands to fulfill my own needs and desires! I have trained them to do what I want them to do. Now, I want to give them back to you. Oh, God, in the midst of all of this suffering, human misery, and hopelessness show me what I uniquely need to do to be of greatest meaning. What can I do, Lord, as your servant, as your hands, to make a difference in such a place as this? Lord, I am yours as I never have been yours before. Would you have me to become a doctor, Lord, and put my life here in the midst of so much suffering and need? Here I am, Lord; use me."

I sat there for the longest time and thought, here I am, a missionary. To many people, being a missionary in an overseas land is the very epitome of servanthood. Just by going to an overseas field is the exercising of the very ultimate in Christian commitment and service, some may think. Not so! The missionary can be as ineffective, meaningless, and careless about life as can the average church member in the pew of a church in America or anywhere else. The surrender of one's life to be a missionary indeed is an act of faith and commitment. However, it is only a first step in a long series of steps. Acts of commitment have to continue throughout the remainder of life. Geography and vocation have little to do with it, except as the arenas of life which provide teachable moments.

I recalled a day several years before in 100-degree heat hauling chairs and benches to an athletic field, nailing together a platform, and walking all over town giving out tracts and leaflets inviting people to our evening, outdoor service. At the end of the day, before the service began, I was exhausted, gulping down a glass of cold tea, thinking, "I thought being a missionary was such a high, glorious calling to be a holy saint of God. But this, this is just pure, unadulterated hard work!"

Now, here I sat outside a hospital room in the midst of human disease, suffering, and despair asking new questions about life and the meaning of being a missionary. In that moment I made a decision. "I am only 33 years old," I said. "I have a good mind and strong body. I have many years of service ahead of me. I will return to the States on furlough and enter medical school to become the finest medical doctor possible. I will return to Vietnam to bring healing and relief to these people." With that I felt that I was lifting up clean hands to God to accompany my pure heart. I later discovered that what I was really doing was finding a way to meet my own need to minister. That was not God's will for my life. How easy losing one's perspective is in the midst of human suffering. Missionaries who would plant their lives in a place of such intensity constantly walk a fine line between two extremes. They can identify with human suffering, injustice, and poverty to such a degree that they become one with such people in their misery and are defeated by it as they lose perspective. On the other hand they can see so much need all about them that they are overwhelmed by it, become hard and unseeing, and make no attempt at meaningful ministry. Somewhere between these two extremes is a place of service which utilizes gifts and skills in a balanced ministry. Most of us weave back and forth between these two extremes.

I was brought out of my meditation by Pastor Thanh softly calling from the door, "Pastor, pastor, the end is near." I entered the room and again felt the oppressive atmosphere. Outside at 11 p.m. the temperature was 90 degrees. The room was like a heated oven. Fatigue and despair were on the faces of all in the room. Mrs. Thanh passed from this life to be with her Lord for all eternity.

Pastor Thanh, scarcely 28 years of age, a student in the seminary, young in the faith, led all of us out of the oppressive atmosphere into new heights of glory and hope as he lifted his voice in a triumphant prayer of victory. What a beautiful and humbling experience for me, a seminary teacher, to see my student gather up all

God had taught him and energize it with his strong faith! Over the next few days, filled with the spirit and power of God, he led his people across that great divide from hopelessness to faith, from deep grief to a sense of ultimate peace, from despair to triumph in Christ. At times, as I listened to him comfort his church members who loved Mrs. Thanh so much, I heard fragments of my lectures and Bible teaching flow gently forth. They were presented in the uniqueness of Vietnamese culture and expression. Even though my teaching was all in the Vietnamese language, it tended to reflect my own American framework. He was able to take these concepts and let them flow through his own being as a Vietnamese with a depth of understanding and caring that I, an American, could hardly hope to achieve in the Vietnamese culture.

In those moments, as I experienced his ministry to all of us, I looked down at my hands and saw them a bit differently. They could not perform a tracheotomy on a 6-year-old boy's throat. They could not take the cancer from a young woman's abdomen. They had, in their symbolic way, been used to help a young minister to become a beautiful, effective servant—ministering not only to himself in a tragic hour of grief but also to others all about him who were searching desperately for a way to deal with grief, suffering, and pain. God did not call me to be a medical doctor. He called others to do that and gave them the appropriate gifts and commitment to perform that task. He called me to be a minister of the gospel and a teacher of young ministers. He gave me unique gifts to do this. For me to do otherwise would be to ignore His perfect will for my life. The experience of Mrs. Thanh's death no longer was just a source of deep grief. It became one of those precious moments of learning!

Sometimes we think of ministry only as those acts of telling someone about Jesus or performing some kind of religious ritual. The Christian knows that every skill he or she possesses is a gift of God. That may be the gift of typing, drawing, athletics, music, carpentry, and a myriad of other vocations. Because these skills are a gift of God, they are treated as sacred and used with utmost care. Every act we do utilizing these skills is a testimony to the power, presence, and caring of a loving God for this world. No Christian can do his or her job carelessly. No Christian can afford to waste such skills. For this reason Christians seek to develop and use their skills as fully as possible as an act of ministry. In essence, Christians bring their hands to the altar and offer them to the Lord to become His hands to fulfill His purpose in the world.

The next question becomes, "Where in the world should I use these hands?" Much of the world never has had an opportunity to know about the joy of practicing the presence of the Lord in daily life. Indeed, much of the world never has heard of Christ. What a changed world we would have if committed Christians were to spread across the face of the earth to learn other languages, customs, and cultures with the purpose of planting lives and ministries there in order to bring a very lost world to know Jesus Christ in His fullest significance!

God calls every person to some kind of ministry. He gifts each person uniquely for the life He calls them to lead. Hands are not clean when they are kept to oneself to fulfill solely the purposes of one's own life. Hands are clean when they have been returned to God's control and are exercising the gifts which He gives. "Who may ascend into the hill of the Lord?" the psalmist asks. "He who has clean hands and a pure heart," is the reply. What a glorious privilege to have clean hands and a pure heart, and to be in the very center of His will doing that which He intends for us to do in the very place that He has called us!

CHAPTER 5

Discussion Questions

Chapter 5 contains a significant dilemma: As followers of Jesus, does our call to serve spring from the human need which surrounds us, or, does the call to serve determine the nature and character of our service to the Lord?

In view of the chapter you have just read, use the following questions to discuss your own pilgrimage as a follower of Jesus.

1. We know that the blood of Christ cleanses us from all of our sins and gives us that pure heart. However, what causes us to have clean hands?

2. This chapter speaks of a fine line between two extremes that the follower of Jesus must walk as he or she serves among the poor, the afflicted, the sick, the hopeless of the earth: On the one hand, faced with such tremendous devastating need, one tries to meet every need. Thus the sheer magnitude of need can cause the loss of all perspective. We can become as hopeless as those we serve. On the other hand, in order to survive in the midst of hopelessness, one simply can turn a deaf ear and a hard heart toward the need and do nothing. How do you keep perspective in the midst of the lostness and human need all about you?

Chapter 6

The Gift of Tu

Three taxis stopped directly in front of our house. I wondered who would be visiting us on a Saturday morning. From our upstairs window I watched as a host of Vietnamese got out of the taxis, formed a line two abreast, and began moving slowly and reverently toward our front door. I recognized them as the families of Pastor Do Vinh Thanh and his recently deceased wife. The procession was led by the two fathers of Pastor Thanh and Mrs. Thanh. Immediately following these two tall, stately men, walking side by side, were the mothers of Pastor and Mrs. Thanh. Walking alone behind the parents was Pastor Thanh himself. Several of his brothers and sisters completed the entourage that numbered 11 persons in all.

The two fathers were dressed in traditional garments worn usually by older Vietnamese men at solemn occasions or special days. They were both dressed completely in black to signify their mourning. The two mothers wore their traditional black Vietnamese dress. Pastor Thanh wore a dark blue business suit with a black armband signifying his state of mourning for his wife. This period of mourning lasts three years for one who has lost a spouse. During this time Pastor Thanh could not have any kind of relationship with a female. The girls in the party wore white traditional dresses with a small black ribbon attached to the left side of the bodice as their symbol of mourning.

As I greeted them at the door, each held up hands clasped in front at shoulder height in a gesture of greeting. They bowed their heads several times as they entered the house silently and rather mournfully. When all were seated, my wife served tea to each. While we drank tea, we engaged in small talk about various, unimportant subjects. I knew that, if I waited patiently, at the right moment their reason for visiting would be revealed.

Shortly after the funeral of Pastor Thanh's wife, at our request, we had taken his 2-year-old son, Tu, to our home to give the pastor a few days to recover from his wife's death. Nearly two weeks had passed since the funeral. My daughter, Deborah, brought Tu downstairs for a joyous reunion with his father and grandparents. My impression was that these two families had visited our home to formally express their appreciation for our keeping Tu during these difficult days. They now would be ready to take him to the home of one of the grandparents. I guessed that Tu probably would go to live with Mrs. Thanh's mother, since she is a wonderful, committed Christian. Pastor Thanh had confided on many occasions that his own father, a pastor in another denomination, in reality was a very explosive, demanding man and was capable of making life very difficult within the family. I knew that if Pastor Thanh had any say in the matter, he would prefer that Tu not live with this grandfather.

During the two weeks that Tu lived with us, we had fallen in love with him. He had beautiful, hazel eyes with unusually long eyelashes. Though he was scarcely more than 2 years old, he already had been taught several short verses of Scripture. My own children had taken him in as a little brother. How we laughed as we watched this brilliant little fellow fight for his rightful place at our family table in the midst of eating, games, and play. Our family members often remarked that we might never want to give him back. Each night, as we prepared for bed, Rachel and I would kiss and love him right along with our own children. In those few days he truly became one of our own. I found myself sitting in the midst of Pastor Thanh's family silently hoping that they had not arrived to take Tu from us.

After the second pouring of tea, Pastor Thanh's father moved forward to the edge of his chair. In typical Vietnamese fashion he did not look directly at me but politely addressed me and then my wife. "We, the two families of us, have had a meeting this morning to discuss the future of my son. He no longer has a wife for himself nor a mother for his son. He is faced with many problems to solve regarding his future. He will not be able to adequately care for his son and do justice to his ministry as pastor. None of us has the financial resources to provide for Tu the kind of life and education that he needs."

He paused for a long time. I looked at my dear friend and student, Pastor Thanh. His face was expressionless. He stared into space as though looking at nothing. In typical Vietnamese fashion he obediently had yielded the floor to his father. I knew that whether or not he liked what his father was saying would make no difference at this point. Whether he disagreed or agreed, he would have to follow his father's wishes. Such is the respect of the traditional Vietnamese for parents. My heart was flooded with compassion for him. It was one of those times when a missionary feels most acutely the clash of his own cultural freedom with what he feels to be the restrictive customs of another culture.

I waited in silence for the old man to continue. He began again with great solemnity and authority.

"We have decided to give the child, Tu, to you. He will become your son. We will give up all claim to him. You will take him to rear as your own. There are several reasons for this." Again, he paused for a long time as he sought to find the right words.

I was grateful for the pause. I felt as though I had just received a violent shock of electricity. Again, I reached out in mind and heart to my dear, young friend. Pastor Thanh continued to sit motionless and stoic. I knew that if he and I were alone, we would have embraced and wept together. Our personal relationship transcended culture and traditional practice. He would be honest with me. I would know his heart, whether he voiced it or not. But now, I must yield to culture and tradition. I forced myself to maintain silence and wait patiently for the Vietnamese sense of timing.

Pastor Thanh's father raised his hand, extended his thumb and said, "First." Americans usually count on their fingers beginning with their forefinger and ending with the thumb to indicate a fifth point. Vietnamese begin counting with their thumb and end their points with the little finger. He held up his thumb authoritatively, saying again, "First of all, we see that you have a truly Christian home. Tu would receive a good religious foundation from you. Second," his forefinger darted the air, "You have more financial

59

resources than my son ever will have. You can provide him with education and physical needs. Third, you are American and, in many ways, you also are Vietnamese. He would have the best of both worlds. You could help him to continue the language of his birth and also give him the English language. Fourth, someday you will take him to America, where he will go to college. Fifth, he has no future in Vietnam. Our country always will be ravaged by war. He someday will be an American living in that land of peace and hope."

With that, he picked up his cup of tea and settled back comfortably in his chair. He never looked at me directly. No one else had spoken a word. I knew it was my turn to speak.

I looked at Rachel. She had the same shocked expression that I knew also must be on my face. Just then, Tu, running across the room, tripped and fell. I jumped from my chair, hugged him close, and set him back on his feet.

Pastor Thanh immediately replied, "Let him pick himself up. He must learn to fall and to get up alone. We never must make him dependent on anyone." It was an awkward moment but a moment fraught with meaning. My closeness with this young pastor helped me to interpret what he really was saying. He was telling me that he loved his son more than anything. He was saying that he was not ready to give up the responsibility of rearing his son. He was saying that the reasons given by his father for giving us his son were not really valid reasons if Tu were to ever become his own person.

I returned to my seat and sipped tea quietly for a moment. I knew that giving an answer immediately or even on that day would not be appropriate. To say "no" would have been extremely impolite. To say "yes" so quickly would have given the impression of treating the matter too lightly.

I replied that we counted it a great honor to be chosen to bear such a great responsibility. I said, "My wife and I love Tu as we have loved his father and his mother." I continued, "It is such a great responsibility that we need to pray and earnestly seek God's will." I inquired whether they would give me permission to wait for a few days to give our reply. The old man graciously consented.

At that point the atmosphere seemed to relax. After a few moments of conversation on other subjects Pastor Thanh's father stood. On behalf of both families, he expressed appreciation for our entertaining them in our home. He then asked permission to leave. I again described my pleasure at the honor of their visit. Rachel and I followed them out to the waiting taxis. Tu remained with us and seemed perfectly happy to wave good-bye to his family.

The next two days were filled with intense emotion and inner turmoil. To our family, prayer became like breath itself. Rachel and I knew what was best for Tu. Our heads said for us to return him to his father. Our hearts said for us to keep him and love him as one of our own. We wrote out all of the reasons for keeping him and all of the reasons for returning him. In this situation we knew from the beginning what we must do. We simply had to struggle out of deep emotion of the heart and decide out of a conviction of God's will.

Two days later Rachel and I packed Tu's belongings and drove to Pastor Thanh's home. The pastor's elderly father, along with several other family members, were there. Again, we drank tea and talked of several incidental matters. Then I moved forward in my seat. I began by explaining our joy at having kept Tu in our home since the funeral. I recited all the events of the past few days. I described our feeling of humility and honor at being chosen to be Tu's parents. However, I could see many reasons why Tu would do better continuing under the nurture and care of his father.

I waited a few moments to let them ponder this. When I began to speak again, I began to weep. This was very uncharacteristic of the Vietnamese way and custom. Grief and emotional strain had drained my energy so that I could not control the need to express the depth of my heart. The entire family began to weep with me. This seemed to give us all an opportunity to free up the intense pent-up feelings. In fact, evidently this was one of the few times that the family members had been able to weep together since the funeral and to express their deep sense of loss at the death of their precious loved one.

After a period of weeping and talking about Mrs. Thanh, the elderly father said to me, "I understand. We accept your decision."

During the entire conversation, I watched Pastor Thanh as closely as I dared. We understood each other so well that neither of us needed to speak. Our relationship had many faces. I had been his teacher and he my student. I had been his pastor and he my parishioner. I had been his pastoral supervisor and had gradually turned the church, which we had started together, over to him. Perhaps more importantly, our relationship had developed into a warm friendship, which endured all the stresses of cultural variation, distinct personality differences, and marked economic variances. These differences no longer seemed important in light of our easy friendship.

Together we had been through danger. As I looked into his face, I could not help remembering how, as recently as a month before, he had been in grave jeopardy with communist soldiers. That night I had conducted a prayer meeting in his church—a simple bamboo structure with a thatched roof of banana leaves. We said good-bye; I left to return home. Pastor Thanh remained at the church with several young church members.

Scarcely had I left when eight communist soldiers burst into the church. They placed a chair in the center of the room and forced Pastor Thanh to sit in it. The young church members were forced at gunpoint to lie face down on the floor. Several soldiers began to walk around and around the chair. They pointed their fingers at Pastor Thanh and occasionally slapped him in the face.

They first accused him of being a slave to an imperialist American. To the communist soldiers all religion is a foreign religion. Their favorite saying was, "To follow Buddhism is to follow decadent forces in Asia. To follow the Catholics is to follow the French. To be a Protestant Christian is to follow the Americans. To be a communist is to be a true Vietnamese." They accused him of selling his soul to the Americans. He now was a "puppet" of American imperialist forces.

After an hour of their constant accusation and unsuccessful efforts to get him to "cleanse" himself with a confession, they began a rapid barrage of questions. According to the later testimonies of the teen-age church members, every question received the same answer from the pastor. To each successive question, he replied over and over again, "I know nothing but Jesus Christ and Him crucified."

They asked, "What does the American missionary say about us?" "What does he say when he preaches?" "Why do you insist on following him?" As the hours went by, the atmosphere became more intense. They circled his chair and poked at him with guns. Then, in the early hours of the morning, just before light began to dawn, they left as suddenly as they arrived. They made one parting statement: "Stop following that American religion, or we will return again." From that day forward, Pastor Thanh never wavered from his faith. The realization that God had divinely spared his life simply increased his faith.

The next day he visited our home to implore me not to visit the church for a while for my own safety. He knew that the communists were prepared to take my life as well as his. This experience bonded us together with a special, lifelong bond of friendship and mutual faith.

After I had told the group our decision about Tu, Pastor Thanh continued to sit silently. However, his entire body had relaxed. The spell which his father seemed to have cast over him now was gone. His face radiated a smile. He did not say a word, but I knew that among his thoughts was the determination that by the grace of God he was going to rear his son.

As Rachel and I threaded our way home through streets teeming with motorbikes, cars, trucks, ox carts, horse-drawn wagons, and pedestrians, neither of us wanted to talk. Inwardly, we kept asking, "Have we done the right thing?" Just moments before, Tu had sat excitedly in the seat between us. Now the car seemed sadly empty.

Being caught in the middle never is pleasant. In this experience I was caught between my own culture and that of my Vietnamese pastor friend. I was caught between my love for Tu and my love for his father. I was caught between my joy at having Tu join our family and the grief of sending him away to a home void of a mother. I was caught between the desire to give that young life all the hope and potential that my American identity could give him and the realization of his questionable future in a war-devastated land. I was caught between my heart conviction that as his new father I somehow could give him more than his own father could and the intellectual conviction that his own father, no matter how wounded, has the potential of loving his son with a love unequaled by anyone. Knowing when one has made the right decision never is easy. One only can be certain that the decision was made with the best light available and with the assurance of God's leading.

Perhaps the very nature of the Christian life is to be constantly caught in the middle. We live out our lives in a secular world with secular values while we try to live a life influenced by Christian values. We constantly live in a world which relies on the technology and wisdom of humankind, yet we know that God's power transcends all of this. We constantly face the conflict between what belongs to culture and what belongs to the essence of the gospel. We seem to be born with a philosophy which says, "I want what I want when I want it." Much of our personality and behavioral patterns are determined in the tension between self-gratification and self-discipline. Certainly, taking Tu into our home would have been gratifying, but we have no doubt that the greater decision would be to nurture the love between a father and a son.

We would have a poor life indeed if we never were enriched by taking risks which afford opportunities to make decisions. To make the wrong decision in life provides an unparalleled opportunity to learn and to grow. To make the right decision enriches the life and affirms the process.

Jesus put it best when He said, "For whoever wishes to save his life shall lose it, but whoever loses his life for My sake, he is the one who will save it" (Luke 9:24). Always within us is that desire for self-preservation, yet the gospel calls for a faith commitment to an unknown future which lies in the hands of a loving Savior. That means taking a risk, which inevitably will involve significant decisions.

CHAPTER 6

Discussion Questions

This chapter contains several significant dilemmas: One is the decision, when faced with a dilemma, whether to follow the mind or the emotion of the heart when the two are in conflict. Another is the problem of the old, traditional culture of parents versus the more modern culture of a son who himself is caught emotionally between the two. Another dilemma is the author's desire to guarantee a long-term, hopeful future for the little boy versus the desire to preserve the father/son relationship even in face of an uncertain future.

In view of the chapter you just read, use the following questions for discussion regarding your own spiritual pilgrimage as a follower of Jesus:

1. What do you do when you are caught between the emotions of the heart and the reasonable logic of the mind?

2. Put yourself in the author's place. Would you have accepted the gift of Tu?

3. What does this story say about a missionary learning language, establishing close relationships, and understanding culture?

Chapter 7

Mr. An's New Life

He made his way rather quickly down the aisle as soon as the hymn of invitation began. As was the custom at the Vietnamese Grace Baptist Church in Saigon, the pastor always gives an invitation after the sermon in order to provide everyone with an opportunity to make a decision of some kind regarding what each person has heard. This man did not hesitate as most did but stepped out decisively and walked the aisle as though something impelled him forward. When I reached out to take his hand, he rather hesitantly extended his hand with his fingers closed as in a fist. He was a small man—about five-feet-three-inches tall and extremely frail. As he shared his decision, I had to bend down to hear him. He haltingly said simply, "I need to become a new man."

I had preached the sermon that morning on a text in 2 Corinthians, chapter 5, verse 17, which says, "Therefore if any man is in Christ he is a new creature; the old things passed away; behold, new things have come." I invited him to remain at the front until the service was over so we could talk about his decision. He then sat down on the front pew to await the completion of the hymn and my introduction of him to the congregation. The only information he wanted to give to me at this point was his name, Mr. Nguyen Van An, and the fact that he wanted to accept Jesus Christ as his Savior and to become a new man.

As I introduced him to the congregation, he stood with head bowed. He never looked at the people. This was not entirely unusual for the Vietnamese, as it demonstrates proper dignity and humility. However, with Mr. An, he seemed to be hiding his face. I watched as people moved to the front of the church to greet him and to assure him of their love and prayers for him. He seemed to avoid personal contact.

I found myself a bit uncomfortable and wondered who this man actually was. Many strangers were present in church every Sunday morning. Seldom did a first-time visitor make a public decision during the invitation hymn. While I preached, I had spotted Mr. An in the congregation. He sat next to the back row on the end of the pew. As I preached, I found myself focusing my attention on him. His eyes reflected an unusual interest in what I was saying, as though he was clinging to each word. I always try to watch closely the faces of members of the congregation while I am preaching in order to have a sense of whether they are understanding or not. The expression on his face was one of understanding. Yet it was an expression of sadness, or fear, or anxiety which I could not define. A bit of fear of him stirred within me as I preached. His eyes seemed cold and gray.

When everyone had exited the building, I sat with Mr. An to counsel him about his decision. As I counseled him, I searched his face and eyes for some impression of who this man was. The lines in his face were etched deeply. Occasionally, when he smiled, deep wrinkles forming a constant frown all but disappeared and were replaced with deep "crowfoot" wrinkles at his eyes. His skin was like leather, as though it had been exposed for years to the elements. The color of his skin was not a healthy color but rather a pale yellow tone.

I suddenly realized that my fear emerged from looking at his eyes. Instead of the usual brown or hazel of most Vietnamese, his were almost gray and cold, like steel. While I talked with him, I experienced almost a paradox. A feeling of strength and power exuded from him. At the same time I sensed brokenness and sadness. "Who is this man?" I kept saying to myself.

He gave me his address and suggested I wait until the following Sunday to visit his home. I agreed not to visit that week and bade him farewell. All week long I could not free my mind from the compelling face of this man.

The following Sunday before the service I stood near the door leading into the sanctuary. I could hardly wait for him to arrive. At the last moment I made my way to the podium to begin the service.

All morning I watched expectantly for his arrival. He never showed up.

After the service I approached one of the deacons and suggested that the two of us visit Mr. An that afternoon. As we drove to Mr. An's home, I hardly could contain the tremendous conflicting feelings raging inside. I almost dreaded the moment we would arrive at his house. His eyes, the paleness of his skin, the sad expression of his face, the demeanor with which he greeted the church and me, all set up a sense of fear or dread. Yet, my heart wanted to reach out to him more than anyone I ever had encountered in all of my years in Vietnam.

The address he gave was almost impossible to find. We parked on a main street and began walking through the narrow alleyways that wound for more than a half mile among small, temporary houses, which were little more than wooden or tin shacks. We stopped frequently to ask directions. I always felt strange in the back alleyways amidst the rows of houses built of everything from pasteboard boxes, scrap plywood, wooden crates, pieces of tin, and a variety of other materials to be found here and there. Foreigners did not venture into some of these areas, so Vietnamese were surprised to see someone with brown hair, round eyes, and pale skin walking through. Only once did I feel afraid in such an area, however. That was a time when we gave out gospel tracts. The people, particularly the children, mobbed us and tried to take tracts from our hands. We simply could not give them out fast enough. When I gave out all of the tracts, the crowd became even more unruly. I had to run out of the maze of alleyways to keep from being hurt unintentionally by the crowds.

As usual I could feel the eyes of many people watching as I went by. Most watched out of a deep curiosity. Others watched out of suspicion. The Vietnamese people are by nature a friendly people, but years of war and struggle for survival caused them of necessity to be cautious.

Children ran along behind pointing and shouting "*My, My, My*" (pronounced *Mee, Mee, Mee*, and meaning *American, American, American*). Occasionally I would grin at the Vietnamese deacon at my side, turn around, and say to the children, "Yes, I am an American, but I belong to Jesus Christ. He is my Savior and Lord." With that we would hear peals of laughter at this stranger who spoke Vietnamese.

We continued along the alleyways. We picked up more children along the way and lost some as they turned to go back home to pursue more exciting games. By the time we reached the area where Mr. An lived, no more children followed. In fact, in this area, everything was strangely quiet.

The houses here looked a bit more permanent. Small, low, bamboo fences ran along the front of each tiny yard. Hibiscus plants grew up through the bamboo and made an attractive hedge. Here and there bougainvillaea ran along the front edge of a porch. It gave a beautiful splash of red, orange, or purple to what might otherwise have been a drab scene.

We finally reached the address Mr. An gave us. Several young men played a game in the street. We pushed open the small gate and called into the house. Because of the oppressive heat the door and all shutters were open. After we called several times, we saw that no one seemed to be at home. Leaving the deacon at the front gate I sought out the oldest-looking young man. I asked him if a Mr. An lived there. From the expression on his face, I saw some recognition but also a hesitancy to reply. I asked a second time and heard an immediate, "No!" He turned to leave. I called again, "Please, I am a pastor. Mr. An is my friend. He visited our church last week. I must find him."

He stopped, turned around, stepped very near, and whispered, "Mr. An is my uncle. He has been a Viet Cong (communist) guerrilla for many years. He turned himself in to the police last Monday and now is in a detention center." I asked, "Where is he in detention?" The young man replied, "I do not know, but I think he is in Chi Hoa prison."

The elderly father of one of our young pastors worked for the Vietnamese government with the group called "Returnees." These are Viet Cong who have given themselves up to the government. We immediately visited this man and enlisted his help in finding

Mr. An. Later we learned that Mr. An indeed was in prison. He had turned himself in to the government the morning after he trusted Christ as his Savior. As much as six weeks might pass before he would be allowed time out of detention.

The passing weeks seemed like months. Every Sunday I searched the faces in the congregation to see if he was there. Then one Sunday as I entered the pulpit, I saw him seated on the front row. His face glowed with a big smile. The previous signs of stress seemed to have disappeared. He now had a kindly expression as he looked toward me. He evidently struggled with the singing of hymns but genuinely tried to sing. After the service he approached me and immediately wanted to tell his story.

I sat enthralled and clung to every word. He was born in the western part of Vietnam near the Cambodian border. As a young man he was trained in the northern part of Vietnam before the French were defeated and the country was divided between north and south. He was trained to be a "political commissar" for the communist party. This meant that his job would be to teach communism. He eventually was assigned to teach in the villages along the Cambodian border. For many years he faithfully had served the communist cause. He said that he had reached the point at which he could kill for almost no reason at all, so long as the end result would further communist ideology.

Several years ago he discovered white spots on his hands. Medical doctors confirmed his worst fears. He had leprosy. His fingers now already were disfigured. This explained his reluctance to shake hands and his unusual avoidance of people. After some treatment his leprosy now was dormant. However, several months ago he was diagnosed as having tuberculosis. He began to grow weak and unable to travel in the jungles and rural countryside any longer. His disease had advanced to the point at which his health was severely damaged. He received no help whatsoever from his superiors. In fact, at one point when he was seriously ill, his comrades abandoned him to die in the jungle. Lying alone in that condition his hopes and dreams of a new society united under one true ideology were shattered. He believed that all of his life he had been used

70

as though he were a machine. When he no longer was usable, he was cast aside like junk. He was thoroughly disillusioned. During this experience he realized that if he were to survive, he must get to a place at which medical assistance was available.

Using a false identification card he made his way into the city of Saigon. He got admission to a government hospital and received treatment. His recovery was remarkably fast. He sent for his wife and gradually returned to health. On the first day out of the hospital he was walking past Grace Baptist Church on one of the major thoroughfares in Saigon. He heard the singing of hymns. This caused him to stop. His mind went back 40 years to the time he was a very young man visiting Hanoi. One Sunday a relative had taken him to a Protestant church. There he had his first exposure to Christianity. What he remembered most about that Sunday was the singing. It was a pleasant memory. It was only one Sunday, but this memory lasted him a lifetime and ultimately helped to change his life.

He told how on hearing the singing in Grace Church, he stood outside for several minutes. He felt as though a giant magnet was drawing him into the church. On that Sunday he learned that he could become a new man. Indeed, he became a new creation in Christ Jesus.

Mr. An and his wife became the most faithful members of Grace Church. The same total commitment he had given to communism he now gave to the church. One evening as we sat talking, he reflected on a comparison between the communist methodology of communication and the Christian methodology. He said that he had begun to understand the theology of the church quite well. He described it as being very similar to communism in that the church is a classless society similar to the society found in communist ideology.

"However," he said, "the church is ignoring human nature. You expect professionals and working classes, rich and poor, to immediately embrace each other and enjoy mutual acceptance. This ignores the prejudices of humanity."

He continued to tell how historically the communists have had to intervene in society to destroy these classes in order to attain a classless society. The rich and the professional classes must be brought low. Humankind cannot live without prejudice. Only when the masses understand this can peasants and working classes accept those formerly in other classes of society.

"Only by long-term education and by force can this happen in an Asian society," he said. "In the church," he continued, "force is unacceptable. Therefore, intense education in the teaching and spirit of Jesus is the only acceptable answer." He said, "I see that only in Christ can humankind, of its own will, put aside its differences, prejudices, and contention in order to establish in a natural way a just and united humankind. Christ is the only way to redeem humankind," he said emphatically.

Mr. An then presented a plan about which he had thought for some time. He wanted to combine the most effective methods of the communists with the power of the gospel. He told how that for years as a political teacher he would gather people of like interests and like vocations together to give them intense indoctrination.

"For example," he said, "in Saigon the communists have cell groups made up entirely of taxi drivers. Only taxi drivers can attend. The same thing is true for lower-class industrial workers. It also is true for professionals." He then proposed that we point our evangelistic efforts toward these separate, small groupings of people. On Sunday mornings they may be able to join together with all elements of society and form a powerful, united people for the sake of Christ.

"This will only happen, however, when people of like mind and level in society are intensely taught separately, then brought together to practice the mind and spirit of Christ," he explained. "In this way," he continued, "you are working within the mindset of Asian people and at the same time accomplishing the goals of the church in Christ Jesus."

Just days after he shared that important missiological insight, a tragic thing happened. Early one morning we were awakened by an insistent knocking at our door. I looked out of the window and saw Mrs. An evidently quite agitated. A taxi waiting for her was parked in front of our house. I hurriedly opened the door and invited her in.

She broke into tears, exclaiming, "Pastor, pastor, my husband wants you to go to him quickly. I fear he is dying. He has been so sick. His fever is extremely high. Please hurry." I dressed quickly and followed her to their home. When I arrived, people were bringing Mr. An out on a cot to place him in a taxi. I rushed to his side. He looked up at me with a beautiful smile. His voice was weak and hardly audible.

"Oh, pastor, I wanted to see you so badly before I leave," he said. I knelt in the dust on the side of the road beside him. "Brother An, where are you going?" I asked. He whispered, "I am going back to my home village to die. My time is here."

Then, his voice growing weaker with each word, he gently gripped my hand and said, "I regret that I only lived for three years. I am 58 years old, but I did not begin living until I met Jesus. Thank you for telling me about Him." These were the last words I ever heard him speak. He died in the taxi before he could reach his home village.

I drove the 12 kilometers back to my home in Thu Duc, north of Saigon. The tears kept blurring my vision. Time and again I had to pull over to the side of the road to keep from having an accident. Only in Christ can someone like me, a "rich American" as the Vietnamese consider us, and someone like Mr. An, a former ardent communist, learn to love and respect each other. In the midst of warfare on every hand, I was able to learn to love genuinely and sincerely this man who for so long represented the "enemy." He was a poor man, a broken and defeated man, a one-time "enemy", but God broke down the walls that divided us. Through His redeeming grace he made the two of us to walk together in peace. We loved each other as brothers in Christ, Mr. An and I.

CHAPTER 7

Discussion Questions

This chapter presents a significant dilemma: When a person who has committed himself to literally years of anti-religious teaching and even taking the life of any number of people says, "I want to become a new creation", do you believe that this can happen and trust that it is happening? Or do you keep your distance and wait for the person to prove himself or herself?

In view of the chapter you just read, use the following discussion questions as you look at your own pilgrimage as a follower of Jesus:

1. In view of this story and given the life of Mr. An, can we say that anyone ever is beyond the ability to receive Jesus Christ as Lord and Savior and to be saved?

2. Do you believe that prejudice is present in some form in all people? Do you have any prejudices?

3. Can someone overcome prejudice aside from the re-creation that happens when Christ enters that person's life?

4. What did Mr. An mean when he said, "I regret that I only lived for three years"?

5. Can you apply Mr. An's missiological plan in your people group, church, group? How would you do it?

Chapter 8

Mr. Hai's New Hope

"Pastor, I want you to go with me to meet a man who is in great need of ministry," the deacon said. "Certainly," I replied. Nothing thrilled me more than to have a Christian friend concerned about another and wanting me to visit with him.

"This is not an ordinary visit, pastor," he continued. "In fact, I never have met anyone who may be more difficult to talk with. Honestly, I do not know what will happen when we meet him face to face."

This caused me to want to go even more. During those days in Vietnam every challenge seemed to be a power encounter between God and the forces of evil. What a source of rejoicing to see over and over again with my own eyes the victories won through allowing God's power to work simply and efficiently.

"Well," I replied, "let's go right now before something happens to rob us of this opportunity."

In the car on the way to the man's home, the deacon explained what he knew about the situation. This man was hopelessly crippled. He had the use of his arms but no use of his body from the waist down. He spent most of his hours in a wheelchair. Each of his legs had been outfitted with braces, which enabled him to stand for short periods of time. With the braces making his legs stiff and with the use of crutches, he could move himself along by dragging his legs. As he moved along, he swung his body and with delicate balance propelled himself slowly forward. The young man had complained that he felt pain in his back, arms, and neck at every moment. The rest of his body from the waist down had no feeling at all.

"How did he get this way?" I asked. The deacon said that he had heard the story but believed that if the opportunity arose, we would let the man tell the story himself. He did say the man had been in a tragic accident. Whatever happened caused him to be filled with hatred for every person, particularly the communists. He was so embittered that he hardly could speak a word without cursing. Recently, he had become so depressed that his mother was afraid he might either take someone's life or take his own. He had been talking continuously about suicide.

A friend of the deacon was familiar with the situation and begged him to find a way to help this unfortunate man. This deacon had visited with him but recognized right away the hopelessness of the situation. This man was not disposed to receive help from anyone. The deacon said, "Perhaps because you are a foreigner, he might respond to you, especially since you speak our language." He continued, "He looks on Americans as friends, since they are here helping Vietnam in the war effort. He sees communists as his greatest enemy."

I replied, "You know how I do not like to be associated with the idea that I'm here in Vietnam to fight communism. You know I'm here to lead people to know Jesus Christ and be saved. I appreciate my fellow countrymen who are making tremendous sacrifices here, but I must maintain my identity in Jesus Christ and Christ alone. Never do I want Christianity to be seen as an American religion. Never do I want Christianity to be seen as a 'crusade against communism.'"

This was a constant tension in Vietnam. Some people saw every American as being connected in some way with the United States government or the American military. Vietnamese who appreciated the American presence in Vietnam would welcome any American. Those who questioned the presence of American involvement in the war would question the presence of any American, whatever the reason for being there. This meant that the missionary must constantly live so openly and so deliberately show the Christian life and commitment that no mistake would exist as to why he or she was in Vietnam. A part of my own internal struggle as an American was tied into my tension between a great love for my own country and patriotism toward it and my love for Jesus Christ and the

Vietnamese people. I wanted with all my heart for them to believe in Him and be saved. On the one hand, I never could bring myself to completely disassociate myself from my own countrymen. On the other hand, my very presence in Vietnam was by the divine call of God and through His claim on my life.

We arrived in the vicinity of the crippled man's house. We turned off the main road onto a small one-way street, barely wide enough for one car to pass. After what seemed an eternity we finally stopped in front of a very poor dwelling. As we approached the front of the house, I heard a loud noise inside. Clearly someone was extremely angry. He was speaking so loudly and so fast that I could not comprehend what he was saying. I wanted to turn and run back to the car.

I asked my deacon friend, "Do you think we ought to visit some other time?" "No," he said. "He is always like this. We will have no better time." Reluctantly, we called his name through the open door. "Mr. Hai. Mr. Hai, are you at home?"

The noise suddenly subsided. An interminable silence followed. He then appeared at the door. He was on crutches and bent almost double at the waist. His face was contorted with what appeared at first to be hatred and hostility. Later, I realized it was probably as much from uncontrolled pain as from hostility. His hair hung long over his neck and fell across his forehead. It nearly covered his right eye. His clothes were quite neat in spite of his crumpled posture. He had to twist his head at a strained angle to look up at us.

"What do you want?" he demanded. The deacon immediately replied, "This is my pastor whom I told you about. I promised I would bring him here to meet you. I think he can help you."

"No one can help me; I already have told you that!" he growled. I stepped forward and softly spoke to him. "You are right. I cannot help you. Maybe no person on earth can help you. But I know someone who can. He is here with me now," I said.

Mr. Hai looked out toward the car and around the yard. He asked, "Who is with you? Where is he?" "Well," I said, "if you will let us in, I will introduce Him to you." He opened the door and gestured for us to enter.

The room was sparsely furnished. A table with four small stools was there. A picture of the late former Vietnam president, Ngo Dinh Diem, hung on the wall. The structure of the house was sturdier than that of many houses I had visited. I was surprised at the clean tile on the floor and plaster on the walls. At one time it evidently had been a fine house. Along one wall was a table with a bowl, two candles, and a worship altar hanging above it. Hanging just under the worship altar was a picture of an elderly Vietnamese gentleman. Incense sticks, partially burned, stood in a brass vase. A small bunch of bananas lay in the bowl just in front of the incense sticks.

In the back of the room was a kitchen, which led to a small open area in the back of the house. An elderly woman squatted on the floor and washed vegetables in a pan. She did not speak nor did she look up at us. Evidently she had been involved in an argument and had no desire to entertain quests.

Mr. Hai preceded us into the room. He moved along by placing both crutches about 18 inches in front of him. He then would swing his whole body forward with both feet landing firmly in front. Once steadied he repeated the placement of the crutches; thus propelling himself along. I noticed that the braces on his feet ran from beneath his specially made shoes all the way to his waist.

An old wheelchair was in the room. He paused briefly, turned, and fell backward onto the wheelchair. The deacon pulled the small stools from under the table. We sat down.

An awkward silence occurred as though no one knew what to say or how to say it. Finally, noticing the picture of the elderly man at the worship altar, I asked if that was his father. "Yes," he replied. Again there was silence. "Is the woman in the kitchen your mother?" I asked. "Yes," he replied with no further information offered. I thought to myself that this would be a very short visit at this rate.

"Mr. Hai," I said, "As I look at your father's face in the picture, he looks like a fine man." He replied, "He was a university professor. He was a good man."

"I assume he is dead?" I asked.

"Yes," he replied. Another long silence occurred. In an effort to identify with him, I said, "My father died of cancer two years ago. I miss him very much. I think I can understand how you must feel now."

Quickly he replied, "No, you cannot. Cancer cannot be prevented. It is a part of nature and fate. My father was brutally murdered. He was taken from us suddenly without warning." I noticed that the lines across his forehead suddenly grew deeper. A frown cut deeply above his eyes. What once was a scowl now became a frightfully grotesque face, which made me want to look away quickly.

"Mr. Hai, I do not want to intrude on your privacy or be impolite, but I would like to know what happened to this good man." I felt it might be easier for him to begin talking about his father than about himself.

He sat perfectly still and looked at the floor for what seemed an eternity. I knew that this was a crucial moment in the conversation. Either this would lead us inside of him and the visit would be fruitful, or he would close us out and it would end here.

Suddenly, and with great anger, he blurted out loudly, "Do you see my body? Do you see my useless legs? I should have died with my father. All of us would be better for it!" He sat there with clinched fists. He was breathing in rapid, shallow gasps.

"I hate them! I hate them!" he cried. "They are all animals!" His face fell into his hands. I wanted to reach out and touch his arm, but I did not want to risk turning him away. I had not yet earned the right to comfort him.

Then, he looked directly into my eyes and said, "Do you really want to know what happened?" "Oh yes, Mr. Hai, more than anything. Please tell me," I urged.

"It happened almost two years ago," he began. "Our family was doing well. My sister passed her second baccalaureate exam and was admitted to the faculty of law at the University of Saigon. I was already a third-year student in science. My father was a highly respected university professor. We never lacked for anything. This was a beautiful house, which my father bought for our family. One night we were lying asleep in our beds. My father and I slept on a bed against that front wall. My mother and sister slept in the back in a little side room my father built.

"About three o'clock in the morning a terrible explosion occurred. It knocked the entire front wall into the house. When I regained consciousness, a large section of cement blocks was lying on top of me. I could not breathe. I called for my father, but he did not answer me. Everything was totally dark. My ears were ringing. I wondered if I was blind and deaf. Soon someone arrived with a lantern. Flashlights began to shine everywhere. I kept calling for my father.

"I then became aware of someone holding my head. In the lantern light I could see the face of my sister. She was crying and trying to hold me close. Through the terrible ringing in my ears I could hear her muffled voice saying, 'Father is dead. Father is dead.'

"I did not remember anything after that, until I awakened in the hospital. The first thing I tried to do was to get out of the bed, but my legs would not move. You cannot know how I felt to realize for the first time that I could not move! Days later I learned what happened.

"At the end of our street is a Vietnamese military compound where vehicles are parked and gasoline is stored. The vehicles are brought there for repairs and servicing. A high wall is all the way around it. A small group of Viet Cong (communist) terrorists had a mission to blow up the fuel storage tanks and destroy all of the vehicles. They began to scale the wall. An army guard spotted them and opened fire. They all turned to run down our street. As they passed our house they threw a satchel of explosives against our front wall. It immediately exploded, sending the entire front wall crashing onto my bed. My father was instantly crushed to death. I only wish I had died with him."

With this, he burst into sobs. His entire body wretched with deep anguish. At that point, I decided to take a risk. I moved to kneel beside him. I put my arm around his shoulders and held him tight. For a long time nothing was said. The only sound in the room was the gradual, subsiding sound of his weeping.

He soon straightened himself as far as his paralyzed body would allow and said, "I am sorry. This is the first time I have wept in a long time. I do not like to talk about this. I do not understand why I am talking about it now."

As I looked at him I suddenly realized how vulnerable this fierce-looking man really was. From a violent man who had struck fear and terror in my own heart just minutes before, he now was subdued and broken. My first thought was that what once was like brittle, dry clay had now been moistened with tears and was pliable. Surely the Potter's hands were ready to mold this vessel into a new creation.

I expressed to him how grateful I was that he allowed my friend and me to share in his experience. With that, he suddenly changed again. His face grimaced with anger. I could not believe how bitterness and a sense of absolute evil so quickly could return to manifest itself. Almost at a shouting level he said, "Do you want to know what my real problem is? I'll tell you. Every moment of every day I want revenge. I want someone to pay for this. If I could find one communist, I would use my bare hands and rip him to shreds!"

Again, he was gasping for breath. He continued, broken. "I am helpless. I cannot move. I cannot walk. I cannot search for them. I have no way to get at them. I sit here day after day seething in anger. All I can do is hate everyone, even my mother!"

I decided not to respond but to allow him time to continue to bleed off these long months of pent-up, explosive feelings.

After a long pause, he asked, "Do you want to know what happened to my sister?"

"Yes," I replied.

"She never comes home anymore. She no longer goes to school. Do you know what she is now?" he shouted. "She is a cheap prostitute walking the streets at night. She picks up American servicemen and goes wherever they want her to go, doing what they want her to do."

He continued, "What can I say? If she did not send money to my mother and me we would starve to death. She makes more money on the street in one night than she could make at some respectable job in a month. Do you know how it hurts that I cannot do anything to prevent this?"

81

When Mr. Hai told me about his sister, I could not keep back the tears. I realized that this young woman, reared in the warmth and protection of a beautiful family, in one split-second of a vicious, thoughtless attack had been transformed into a person of the streets. She sold her body to keep a bitter, crippled brother and an elderly mother alive. What tragedy!

Deep in my heart I wanted to cry out, "Oh, God, where are you? Why do these people, a whole nation of human beings, have to suffer like this year after year? Is no end in sight? Where is your mercy?" This was one of those times when my years of university and seminary training did not help. The questions were too many and too profound. The answers were too few and too shallow. I was face to face with the absolute reality of a world without knowledge of the love of God, where sin in the human heart has free reign to bring its destruction and death at will.

At that moment I began to speak. I admitted that I did not have the answers to the difficult questions that he had raised. I did not have the wisdom to explain away all that had happened. I did not have the power to deal with his strong emotions. However, I had something that I wanted to share with him.

"Mr. Hai, I told you that I brought along someone who can help you. Would you give me permission to introduce Him to you?' I asked.

"Yes," he replied with a puzzled expression.

I took out my New Testament and explained what the New Testament is. Then I read John 3:16, "For God so loved the world that He gave His only begotten Son that whosoever believes in Him should not perish but have everlasting life."

"It is this Son that I want you to know," I told him.

His reply was, "What do you mean God loves the world? Do I look like someone that some supernatural being loves? If this is true, I do not want any more of His love!"

I replied that what had happened to his family and to Vietnam had occurred because people refuse to know God or to listen to Him. They do not receive His love. The world fails to acknowledge God's presence; thus, their sin runs rampant. It brings death and destruction all about us. God is not the author of sin. He longs to save us from sin and the tragic consequences of it.

"No one knows these consequences more than you, Mr. Hai," I said. From there I went on to introduce him to Jesus Christ. The more I shared the Bible with him, the more interested he became. He was like a starving man suddenly presented with food. He could not get enough.

Before the visit was over, he had opened his heart and allowed Christ to enter it. He seemed to be looking for a way out of his pent-up anger and mental anguish. Deep in his heart he did not want to continue to carry the heavy burden he had borne for so long. Hearing the good news about Jesus gave him an honorable way to lay down the burden and find welcome relief. He was ready for the Lord. The change was astounding, both mentally and physically. On his face appeared a radiant joy in spite of the constant pain. He begged for someone to visit every day and to teach him the Bible. If ever I saw the evidence of a modern-day miracle worked by the Lord, it was this man's dramatic change.

Unknown to the deacon and me, a further, wonderful miracle was about to happen.

CHAPTER 8

Discussion Questions

This chapter presents several dilemmas: One great dilemma faced in this chapter is whether one takes time to risk spending so much time with a person utterly consumed with anger, bitterness, and outright hostility while all around are three million "normal" people who are just as lost without Christ and who seem far more prepared to receive Christ.

Another significant dilemma is whether to risk presenting the gospel on the first visit amidst fits of anger or wait until a more convenient time when more openness to a witness might occur.

A third dilemma is this: How does one who witnesses to Christ in a situation in which a social/political injustice exists transcend one's own cultural/political bias and present an identity in Christ which overcomes that bias?

In view of the chapter just read, use the following questions as an opportunity to discuss your own spiritual pilgrimage as a follower of Jesus:

1. When, with anxiety and fear, you make a visit to share Jesus with someone, how do you overcome that and gain the courage to continue moving forward?

2. If someone like Mr. Hai can be subdued by the name of Jesus and accept salvation, does anyone exist in any condition who cannot be saved? Have you known anyone similar to this who has been saved?

3. If God changed Mr. Hai so dramatically, how has God changed you since you accepted Christ? If you have not accepted Christ, in what ways would you need to be changed by Christ Jesus?

4. How do you respond to injustices which often result from political conflict? How do you maintain your own cultural identity yet bear witness to salvation in Jesus Christ?

Chapter 9

A New World in Microcosm

At the time of this great miracle, Mr. An, the former communist political commissar who had become a Christian and who later died, was still living and was one of the most faithful men in Grace Church. He always entered the church for worship a bit earlier than anyone else did. His favorite seat was on the second pew from the front on the left-hand side of the auditorium. Without ever having been taught to do so, he would seat himself, hold his body stiffly erect, bow his head, close his eyes, and then pray and meditate until the worship service began. As I sat in the pulpit, my attention always was drawn to him. His face had a beautiful glow, as though the very presence of God flowed through him. I had begun to believe that if I could get Mr. An to pray for something, the Lord assuredly would hear it.

Often, as I looked at him, I wondered for what he was praying or on what he was meditating during those long moments. During some intimate moments he had shared with me his regrets at his many acts against people during his long years with the Viet Cong forces. On one occasion he described how he brutally tortured a villager and, after gaining information from him, had put him to death. Another time Mr. An had helped behead a man and had placed his head on a pole in the middle of the village to warn against following the Vietnamese government. Only in rare moments did Mr. An, in a hushed voice, speak to me of these things. No one in the church ever fully knew this man's history.

The very human part of me wondered how he ever could be free of both the memory and the guilt of these kinds of acts. I always returned to the Scripture that God used to bring Mr. An to his salvation experience: "Therefore if any man is in Christ, he is a new creature: the old things are passed away: Behold, new things have come" (2 Cor. 5:17). This is one of God's clearest promises. The very fact that Jesus went to the cross, took all our sins with Him, and then paid the death penalty for sin assures that even Mr. An can find forgiveness and freedom. The fact of Jesus' resurrection from the dead affirms the fact that in Christ this man, too, was raised from an old life dead in sin to a new life redeemed from sin. What a beautiful, new life God gave to Mr. An!

One day I asked this new Christian, "Mr. An, what do you think would happen to you if your former colleagues discovered that you have forsaken communism and embraced the Christian faith?" He replied unemotionally and simply, "They most likely would kill me."

I followed with another question, "Are you sometimes afraid? Do you at times look over your shoulder to see who is following you? Do you sometimes try to conceal your identity?"

"Absolutely not," he replied. "One day in my new life living openly for Jesus is worth more than a lifetime in my old life. How often I risked my life for a cause that has no hope of eternal consequences! If I die tomorrow, I'll have a glorious life eternally with my Savior. People can take away physical life but never can deprive me of my eternal hope in Christ."

As I sat on the podium thinking on this conversation and waiting for the service to begin, a commotion occurred at the front door of the church. Two deacons were pushing the two front doors open wide. I hardly controlled my joy when I saw slowly appearing in the door, hunched, over his crutches, my new friend, Mr. Hai, paralyzed from his waist down. Having just accepted Jesus as His Savior, he now was eager to attend the worship service.

At first his face reflected that bitter, painful expression that was the trademark of his appearance. He looked up, his head half-cocked to one side because of his paralysis, and surveyed the entire congregation. Anxiety swept through me as I saw again that wild expression on his face. All was deathly quiet. All eyes were fixed on him. Without a word, as though he knew exactly where he was heading, he began his slow, agonizing trip down the aisle. Placing his crutches in front of him he quickly swung his braced legs forward until his feet steadied on the floor. He slowly made his way forward. A rhythmic squeaking of his leg braces was followed by the thud of the crutches as they hit the floor. This intensified the unnatural silence that had descended on the church.

To my surprise he stopped at the second pew from the front and swung himself into the seat next to Mr. An. I was filled with terror when I realized that Mr. Hai for almost two years had longed to find a communist on whom he could take revenge for the terrible bombing which had paralyzed him for life. He had vowed his commitment to kill any communist he could find. Now he placed himself exactly beside a former communist. Mr. An at one time belonged to the same political ideology of those who had set off the bomb taking the life of Mr. Hai's father and destroying Mr. Hai's ability to walk. *Should we have searched Mr. Hai for weapons before admitting him to the church? What if he carried a knife or some kind of weapon? Before becoming a Christian he was suicidal. What if he carried a grenade and desired to sacrifice not only himself but every one else? He had been a Christian only a few days. Had he really changed?* All of these thoughts flooded my mind in those tense moments.

I knew one of our deacons had briefed Mr. Hai about Mr. An's presence in the church. He had not reacted well to the notice that he would be in the same church with a former communist. Mr. An also had been briefed on the events which had occurred in Mr. Hai's life as a result of communist terrorism. We had warned Mr. An that staying clear of Mr. Hai for several weeks would be best. Those of us who knew Mr. Hai knew he tended toward violence and had an explosive personality. None of us knew what might happen when the two men met each other.

Evidently Mr. Hai had determined the location of Mr. An in the church. He deliberately moved all the way down the aisle to sit with Mr. An. This was their first meeting. I watched as the two men looked deeply into each others' faces. I saw a moment of hesitation, as though each was not sure what the other would do. I felt my own body tense and ready to spring forward should violence occur.

Slowly across the face of both men at first crept a slight smile. Then both burst into beautiful smiles. Their faces literally flowed with a countenance of peace. Mr. An spontaneously placed his arm around the shoulders of Mr. Hai and hugged him close. Few actions could be more untypical of the Vietnamese cultural tradition than physical hugging. No one could mistake the returned warmth and acceptance that emerged from Mr. Hai.

The entire congregation silently sat watching this beautiful scene. Two former bitter enemies now sat together preparing their hearts for worship. They sat arm in arm on the same pew sharing the same Bible and hymn book. I could not keep tears from streaming down my face. Before our very eyes was a true miracle of God.

Just when I almost had given up hope that Vietnam ever would find peace and freedom from its continuous suffering, this event occurred. I had watched as the greatest military power on earth amassed in South Vietnam and focused sharply on the strong and capable military power of North Vietnam. Nothing seemed to be lacking as the finest military facilities ever assembled were placed at the disposal of the military forces. Despite all this the only thing that seemed to change was the awareness that things seemed to get worse, not better.

Throughout my years in Vietnam I had been excited about the marvelous aid projects which were carried out. Some of these aid projects helped. Some failed miserably as Vietnamese contractors put just enough aid money into the project to say that it was accomplished while they pocketed the greater part of the funds. This doomed the future value of the project. At first I had thought that while the military forces seemed to be able only to stave off defeat, surely these aid projects could change the thinking of the Vietnamese people. I thought that as they saw America and other friendly countries doing something good for their country, their hearts and minds would change. That did not happen. Instead of changing the people, these projects seemed only to encourage more graft and corruption.

I watched with great hope and interest as America's best diplomats daily sat with the best diplomats the communists had to offer.

These people's jobs were to find an acceptable way to bring peace to Vietnam. These were reasonable men and women. All of them had a personal investment in seeing peace occur. True—two distinct and strong ideologies confronted each other, but since discussions occurred in peaceful, quiet diplomacy rather than on the battlefield, I was hopeful. However, I grew disillusioned that human beings can accept compromise enough to effect meaningful decisions. Thus peace never would arrive in Vietnam as a result of these discussions unless one or the other simply gave up in disgust and went home!

Over the years various countries invested huge sums of money in Vietnam to build factories and industry of varying kinds to try to improve Vietnam's economy. Some said the reason the people are sympathetic to communism is because of their miserable economic plight. If they have work and meaning in their work, they will have no need to become communist, the theory went. I hoped that this theory was correct. However, one experience destroyed this idea.

I was visiting an American medical-doctor friend at the sprawling Long Binh Army Base near the city of Bien Hoa, north of Saigon. He was totally disillusioned. I asked him what had happened to depress him so. He told me that several days earlier one of the friendliest and most industrious workers on the base cut himself severely on his side just under the rib cage. This young man had been brought to the clinic to have the wound sewn up. The doctor had kept the man overnight to be sure that no infection would set in. That night they sat and talked for a long time. The young man spoke English well. The doctor learned that the man was from a fairly wealthy family which had managed to get him the job at Long Binh. The next morning the doctor released him from the clinic to return to work. During the day he saw him several times.

That very night a mortar attack occurred on the Long Binh base. Several Americans were killed. After the mortar attack a wave of communist soldiers hit the base. They tried to make their way through the barbed-wire perimeter. Many of these soldiers had been shot to death, their bodies lying entangled in the barbed wire. The doctor and several other medical personnel had retrieved the bodies from the base perimeter. He was astonished to see that one of the bodies had a white bandage on his side just under the rib cage. The doctor realized that this bandage was identical to the one he had placed on his young friend—the worker on the base. His young friend worked on the base during the day, gathered information, marked targets, and then fought as a communist at night! The doctor lamented, "No wonder many of us leave Vietnam saying, 'Whom can you trust anymore?'"

The American doctor had befriended this man, treated him kindly, helped him financially, and then discovered that he had remained his enemy all along. This event reflected so much of the tragedy of the war. No matter what was done from every angle, nothing seemed to make a change in the overall situation in Vietnam.

Then suddenly these two men, Mr. Hai and Mr. An, burst on my sight. They were bitter enemies. Each had deep hurt beyond description. Immeasurable hatred abounded. A gulf between these two men was a matter that nothing could breach. Developing any kind of meaningful and peaceful relationship between these two enemies would seem hopeless.

In so many ways they represented a graphic picture of Vietnam that made the whole situation look so grim. Yet, in the lives of these two men, a miracle occurred. A genuine acceptance of Christ made the difference.

This little church in downtown Saigon at a brief moment in history was a microcosm of what could happen among the people of the world if the gospel of our Lord only could touch them. This is the essence of the Christian faith lived out before our very eyes. What the greatest military machine in the world could not do, the gospel accomplished. What massive infusions of millions of dollars could not do, Christ, the Prince of Peace, did in a moment of time.

As I sat in the pulpit watching this dramatic event unfold, several verses from the prophet Isaiah suddenly burst on my consciousness. Toward the end of his prophecy in chapter 65, verse 17, he begins the beautiful passage about "new heavens" and "new earth." He gives a series of comparisons between the old and the new and vividly describes the changes that God will create. At the end of that prophecy he describes "the new earth":

"The wolf and the lamb shall graze together, and the lion shall eat straw like the ox; and dust shall be the serpent's food. They shall do no evil or harm in my entire holy mountain,' says the Lord" (Isa. 65:25).

The prophet Micah pierced my consciousness with his words of prophecy in chapter 4 verse 3;

". . . Then they will hammer their swords into plowshares and their spears into pruning hooks; Nation will not lift up sword against nation, and never again will they train for war."

CHAPTER 9

Discussion Questions

This chapter presents several inspiring truths: One great truth is that through the power of the gospel of Christ, hostile sides can be reconciled and at peace. Another truth is that God can give to any person, anywhere, anytime, a new life—with new attitudes, with new perspectives, and with a new purpose. Another truth is that this kind of change seldom happens without someone who is totally committed to the Lord becoming an instrument in God's hands to bring the witness and create the possibility.

In view of chapters 6, 7, and 8 you just read, use the following questions to discuss your own spiritual pilgrimage as a follower of Jesus:

1. Can we say that one of the legitimate purposes of carrying the name of Jesus to all the peoples of the world is to bring reconciliation, hope, and peace between individuals and even between conflicting people groups?

2. Can peace on earth ever occur until Jesus, the Prince of Peace, is born in the hearts and minds of humankind in His transforming power?

3. Can you describe a situation in which God has used you, or could use you, to facilitate reconciliation through a strong witness to the saving power of Jesus Christ?

4. Will a mission outreach that primarily uses aid projects and various ministries to human need be sufficient to bring about dramatic change and reconciliation such as is reflected in this story?

5. What would the world be like if a massive witness to the reality of Christ were to occur and a worldwide turning to Christ would happen? What would be some of the effects? What is your place in this?

Chapter 10

When Failure Is So Real

As the years of missionary service in the midst of the pain and suffering of a protracted war passed by, we occasionally felt the need to get away from it all. No place existed in which one could go to escape from the Vietnam War. It was everywhere; it was nowhere. It would arise with sudden speed and violence in the most unsuspecting place and then disappear as quickly as it arrived. On the coast of Vietnam, about an hour and a half by car, was the city of Vung Tau—a beautiful, sleepy little village the French colonialists had developed into a seaside resort many years before. There we often found a moment of respite.

The road to Vung Tau wound through the countryside through rice paddy lands, through orchards, through rubber plantations, through little villages, and dead-ended at the shore of the South China Sea at the heart of the city. Within a few kilometers of town to the north and south were small, unobtrusive hotels offering little other than a good bed on which to sleep and a beautiful view of the ocean with its rugged coast line.

When I first saw the Villa Lisa, I fell in love with it. The fence along the road was draped with bougainvillaea resplendent with its variety of colors. The yard had no grass but was kept clean and neat with a broom. Ten guest rooms were in a small, one-story, motel-like structure. Each room had its own entrance from the veranda; windows faced the ocean. A porch ran the entire length of the facility parallel to the shore. This allowed guests to sit in the shade and enjoy a beautiful view of the ocean. Huge rocks congested the shoreline, so that when the tide was in, it surged through the rocks and covered most of them until it reached the underpinnings of the guest quarters. I thoroughly enjoyed lying in bed at night and hearing the gentle lapping and surge of the tide among the rocks just outside the window. These rocks offered a place to sit and watch occasional ships pass by. At certain times of the day a lonely fisherman would bring his net. Standing silently on the rocks he would watch intently for fish. Spotting several he would skillfully hurl his net into the ocean and drag it in. The net would be loaded with beautiful fish.

Often at night we would sit on the rocks and watch dozens of small fishing boats, with lanterns in their bow, bobbing on the waters until the wee hours of the morning. This was our refuge from the horrors of war which were everpresent on every side. This was the Villa Lisa.

The Villa Lisa was owned by a Vietnamese woman whose husband was a Filipino. The couple did not advertise, because running a motel for business resulted in heavy government taxes. They were content to have a small, regular clientele with whom they personally were acquainted. This meant that a room almost always was available with short notice. No service was offered, though the owners always were available if called on. Occasionally when I was writing training materials for the seminary, I went alone to Villa Lisa, where I could produce volumes of material without interruption.

One day as I prepared to leave for Vung Tau, two secretaries for the seminary asked if they could ride to Vung Tau with me. One had a brother stationed in the army there. She had not seen him for a long time. I could see no problem with that, as long as two of them went. My practice was never to travel alone with a female, especially that distance to the coast. A missionary never can place himself or herself in a position that might jeopardize one's name and honor.

Nearing arrival in Vung Tau one of the two women, Miss Phuong, began to share a very troubling story. Knowing of my training in psychology and counseling she believed that I might be able to help her. I could sense her desperation and invited the two to visit me in the evening and share the story with me. Just at sundown they arrived. We sat on the rocks and watched darkness settle over the shoreline. In that quiet, peaceful setting Miss Phuong told a deeply troubling story which opened to me a whole new perspective on Asia—a perspective which was to trouble me throughout my missionary life in Asia.

Miss Phuong was engaged to a young man who had joined the Vietnamese air force to become a pilot. They had agreed that when he returned from his flight training, they were to be married. On his arrival home for a few days of leave, the two of them took a walk in the cool of the evening. She told how they walked in silence for a long time. She sensed that he was deeply troubled.

They reached a place on the side of the pathway where they could have privacy. He took her hands gently in his and looked deeply into her eyes for what seemed an eternity. He clearly struggled for the right words. He then told her of a vision that he had experienced. As he told of seeing his plane dive into the ground, she could feel his body trembling. He described the vision vividly as though it actually had happened and he had witnessed his own death. He asked her permission to call the wedding off. He said, "Let me fly for two years. Wait for me faithfully during that time. If I get through those two years safely, we will marry immediately."

He continued, "I do not want you to be a young widow, perhaps with my child. Life in Vietnam is too difficult for that. Please forgive me, but things must be this way."

Miss Phuong was moved by his honesty and sincerity. Out of the depths of her love for him she promised him, "You only do I love. I will remain faithful to you forever." He then said, "I want you to promise me this night that you will love me for the rest of your life. When I die, you will join me wherever I am in eternity."

She said, "I wept for the longest time. Part of me did not want to make such a promise. Part of me wanted to promise him, because I did not want to hurt him during these fragile moments that we were together. Another part of me loved him with all of my being. I knew that I never could be happy with anyone else. At that moment I knew that I must make this promise to him." In the quietness of the evening they pledged their love to each other for eternity—yes, even beyond death.

Not quite a year after they made that pledge, the young man was flying a combat mission. His fellow pilots said that his plane was hit by ground fire. The oil line was severed; his plane crashed. His body never was recovered.

Soon after Miss Phuong was notified of his death, he began to appear to her in her dreams. She related how sometimes even during the day he appeared to be drawing her attention to him. She described how she often saw him dressed in his flight suit, standing very still, beckoning her to him. On several occasions he spoke to her and reminded her of his unending love and asking her to reunite with him in the spirit world. At first she reacted to these visions by telling herself that they were just her imagination born of a heart broken with grief. She told how young men at times will ask her to go somewhere with them. One or two times in the two years since his death she consented, but during the entire time she was with them, she believed that someone was watching her intently with eyes she could not possibly escape.

The spirit world is very real to the Vietnamese people, especially those who never have become Christian. Miss Phuong, like countless young people in Vietnam, was brought up to believe that when a person dies, the spirit moves into the spirit world, where it roams about waiting for special opportunities when it can return briefly to the loved ones it left behind. If the spirit has a loved one or a loving family, it has a home and periodically will return to that home on certain days of the year. If the spirit does not have a continuing relationship with someone among the living, it is doomed to wander forever in the spirit world—distressed, lost, weeping, and wailing. The oldest son's responsibility is to provide these opportunities for the spirit to return home by leading the family in rituals. For this reason when a husband and wife have no son, they are greatly disappointed. Much security exists in having at least one son to carry on this ritual. For the first son in a family to become Christian is extremely difficult. This would mean dooming his ancestors to wander lost in the spirit world with no home. The oldest sons seldom can bring themselves to hurt their parents so deeply by embracing the Christian faith. When an oldest son becomes a

Christian, the parents know in advance that when they die, no one will provide that constant home to which their spirits can come. Such was the belief system in which Miss Phuong was born and nurtured. This was her real world.

Miss Phuong told of a recent experience that she had while riding with her sister on the back of a motorbike. They passed a large cemetery. When she looked into the cemetery, she saw her fiancé standing with his arms outstretched and beckoning her to him. She told how for weeks after that incident she could not sleep. This brought her to try to find help.

I asked Miss Phuong if she ever had seriously considered learning about the Christian faith and about Jesus Christ. She said that since beginning to work at the seminary she had developed a great interest. As I talked to her about Jesus, his life, death, and resurrection, and the way Jesus deals with spirits, she was intensely interested. We talked of the victory believers have in Christ Jesus.

However, no matter what she heard or understood, she could not seem to be released from the fear of the spirit world which held her in its grasp.

We finished talking at a late hour. The two women returned to their brother's home. I continued to sit on the shore and reflected on the story I had just been told. I realized as never before that my American theological education had not prepared me well to deal with the reality of the spirit world. While that world may not be real to the Western mind, it is vividly real to the Asian mind. My studies in theology never had dealt with the unseen spirit world. The New Testament is filled with stories of spirits, demon-possession, and the like. Jesus treated them as real and confronted them. Jesus was victorious over these spirits. The tragedy of places like Vietnam is that so little help exists for people caught in that belief system to deal in a healthy way with their fears of the spirit world. That night I determined to look more deeply into a theology which includes dealing with that unseen world which grips millions in fear.

Often in the ensuing months I took every opportunity to read Scriptures to Miss Phuong and to explain to her about Jesus and how victory over spirits occurs through the name and power of

Jesus. By now she was torn between her desire to be free of her fiancé's spirit and her longing to be with him forever. She could not bring herself to break the tie. Though she never admitted it, she clearly also feared offending her fiancé in such a way that he would retaliate against her.

In every way Miss Phuong was a normal young woman. She was a superb secretary. She was not mentally ill. She experienced no other hallucinations. She showed no symptoms of being mentally unbalanced in any way. If she had not related the story to me, I never would have suspected that anything was wrong. This said to me that literally thousands of normal people labor under these fears every day of their lives.

Early one morning I heard an urgent knock at my door. One of my seminary students, visibly shaken, stood outside the gate. As soon as I reached the gate, he told me about a tragic fire which had occurred the night before. Miss Phuong's home had burned to the ground. She lost her life in the fire. I felt as though I had been hit in the pit of the stomach. This beautiful woman with so much life ahead of her, still caught in the clutches of spirit worship, had slipped into eternity.

I immediately went to her home and viewed the charred remains of her humble dwelling. I visited with neighbors to find out exactly what had happened. They told how Miss Phuong's family used a kerosene stove to prepare meals. Like all families in the area hers stored its kerosene containers in the kitchen. The suspicion was that Miss Phuong's sister had bought what she believed to be kerosene from one of the many vendors who sit on the side of the road and sell to passersby. The kerosene or gasoline sold in this way actually had been been stolen from the American military. Someone would hire young boys and girls to sit on the side of every major thoroughfare and sell it at a reduced price to the population. The problem was that one never could be sure what kind of fuel actually was in the container. Miss Phuong's sister, thinking that she was purchasing kerosene, actually was buying jet-propulsion fuel. When Miss Phuong began to prepare the meal, she lit the stove. The jet fuel ignited. It exploded the container of fuel sitting near the stove.

They told how Miss Phuong and her sister dragged their invalid father out the door to safety. They returned to help their ill mother out. By now the house was almost totally engulfed in flames. For some unknown reason Miss Phuong ran back into the house. The roof caved in; she never returned.

During the next days I could not escape the feeling that Miss Phuong had made up her mind to join her fiancé in the spirit world. She coincidentally could have run back into the flames. She also could have had a compelling call emerging from the spirit world of her fiancé from a voice that to her was real. She may have seen her dead fiancé beckoning her to join him. I never will know the truth.

We can shudder at the millions of people without Christ living in a world of fear and anxiety. But to know personally a precious young woman with so much promise of life ahead of her who is under the control of this kind of mindset is almost unthinkable. How tragic to present the truth and power of the gospel but then to realize that the hold on this person is so powerful that she cannot break it! Neither would she allow the power of Christ to deliver her. How even more tragic when that young woman dies without ever knowing the peace of Christ Jesus that surpasses all understanding!

This is the stuff out of which the call to missions becomes real. When I first went to the mission field, I did so because of the masses of people without Christ. With all my heart I wanted to learn the language of these masses. I wanted to identify with them and share the Good News of Christ cloaked in their language and culture. This motivated me during my first term of service. However, what kept me returning to the mission field was not just awareness of the masses. It primarily was the individuals whom I had known personally and who needed the ministry the Lord wants to give them through His servant. Words cannot describe the anguish of mind and spirit when that glorious news is rejected and tragedy occurs.

Miss Phuong had become the personification of what missions is all about. Millions of people just like Miss Phuong exist to varying degrees. Some will believe and be saved if they just have the opportunity. Some will not believe or will be kept from believing by various forces at work. If no one goes to them, then they are all hopelessly trapped in belief systems that provide no peace, no hope of release. None of them will have an opportunity to be free.

CHAPTER 10

Discussion Questions

This chapter presents a serious dilemma. When you cross from your own world and belief system into the world of another culture and belief system, how much of that culture do you accept and realistically face? How much of that culture do you reject and treat as though it does not exist? The spirit world is a primary world-view of many cultures. Does the Western mind go into that culture and simply reject the spirit-world as untrue? Or does the Western mind accept the reality of the spirit-world in the minds of that people and then reckon with it?

In view of the chapter just read, use the following questions as an opportunity to discuss your own spiritual pilgrimage as a follower of Jesus:

1. Do you know people who have a morbid fear of death and to whom life in eternity is to be feared rather than embraced? How do you deal with those people? Do you yearn for them to have the peace that passes all understanding which occurs only through Jesus?

2. Does the experience of failure become like a cancer in the mind which has the potential of destroying your joy and peace in life, or does it become a learning experience which strengthens you for future life and prepares you for what lies ahead?

3. Does the story about Miss Phuong cause you to be more discouraged about the missionary calling and support, or does this story cause you to want to be more involved in praying, giving, and perhaps even more ready to be personally involved in missions?

Chapter 11

What Would You Do?

When one moves across cultural lines to live among people who have different ideas about life, culture, and tradition, making moral and ethical decisions becomes complicated. In the midst of war they are infinitely more difficult.

The need for a new vehicle arose among our personnel in Vietnam. The order was placed; within a couple of months a new Volkswagen microbus was sitting on the Saigon docks awaiting customs approval. When the microbus was ordered, the tax required by the government was minimal. On the very day the microbus arrived on the docks, a new tax law was adopted. This law prescribed that a 100-percent tax on luxury vehicles now would be required. The tax on utility vehicles was minimal. This meant that a Volkswagen microbus costing $12,000 from a dealer could cost $24,000 including the customs tax.

A notice from the Department of Revenue arrived directing us to the customs office to pay the tax on the new microbus. Missionary Herman Hayes and I went to the office. We hoped that since this microbus had been ordered before the new law, we could bring it through customs with minimal tax as we always had done. This was not to be.

We walked into the director's office. He was disarmingly friendly and kind. We announced that we were there to get permission to pick up our new microbus. He said kindly, "I see that you are missionaries." "Yes, we are," I replied, not sure if this recognition was good or bad.

He sat down, took a long puff on his cigarette, and very thoughtfully opened a file. He looked through it for what seemed an eternity. Finally, he looked up with a troubled expression and said, "We have a problem." I replied, "I am sure that it is no problem that

101

a man of your high position cannot solve." He nodded assent to this and then proceeded to describe the problem.

"You see, we have this new tax law. It will have to be applied to your new car. The question has to do with how it is applied," he said, rather matter of factly. He continued, "For example, if this Volkswagen microbus is a luxury vehicle, then I will to have to charge you taxes equal to the cost of the vehicle, which I see was $12,000. In this case the tax charges will be an additional $12,000. However, if this vehicle is determined to be a utility vehicle, then the taxes will not be charged at all. You can drive the car off the dock today. That would be nice, would it not?" he asked.

We quickly replied that this would be nice indeed and that we would be very appreciative.

"Now," he said, "a manual with your vehicle describes your car. I found it in the front pocket with all of your papers. I have it here before me. It describes your microbus as a nine-passenger vehicle. However, I have a manual here in my office from the company. This manual describes a Volkswagen microbus as an eight-passenger vehicle. Here is the problem. Any vehicle which carries nine passengers is a utility vehicle. Any vehicle which carries fewer than nine passengers is a luxury vehicle." Another long silence with several long puffs on the cigarette occurred. "My problem is deciding which information is correct and which I should accept," he stated.

We hastened to reply that of course the manufacturer's manual with the vehicle was the correct information. "Volkswagen microbuses probably vary from model to model," we explained. "Our model certainly has places for at least nine persons." I then described how my wife led a children's choir at church. I said, "On Sunday afternoon she drives a Volkswagen microbus about the city to pick up the little children. We have had as many as 30 children in the bus. Surely this demonstrates the utility purpose of the vehicle," I said, trying to keep from appearing defensive.

"Yes, you have a point," he replied. An unusually long silence followed, as though he was waiting for us to volunteer more information.

"I imagine that you have little children of your own?" he asked.

"Yes, we each have several," Herman Hayes answered. "Do they like to watch television?" he asked. "Surely you have one."

"Yes, both of our families have a television and our children do indeed like to watch it. However, the American Armed Forces television does not cater to children's programs. The Vietnamese television is not well-developed yet," Herman replied.

"My children have been begging me for a television set," he said. "The problem is that I simply cannot afford it. You know we do not make much money in a job like this," he observed.

"I am sure sorry about that," I replied. "Someday television will be good in this country. Your children will enjoy it. Surely you will be able to get one someday," I said.

He then observed, "I hear that the American military P.X. has all kinds of appliances including television sets for sale at a much cheaper price than we can buy on the open market here in the city."

We hurriedly replied, "That may be true. We never have been in the military store. We are missionaries and have no relationship or privileges with the military. We cannot even go into the store, much less purchase something."

"Is that a fact?" he observed. "Well, let's finish our business here. I have little choice but to declare that my information here in the office is the official information. You will need to leave your tax payment for $12,000 here in my office. I will authorize you to pick up your car."

He then asked rather softly, "Do you have anything you would like to say or further information to offer me while we are in my office?" he asked.

"No," we replied, "but do we have a possibility of appeal? We cannot possibly pay the $12,000. That is far more than we can afford."

"Well," he said, "you could appeal to the minister of economics, but he is not likely to change this ruling. Just let me know when you are ready to pay the tax and get your car."

On the way back to the mission office we discussed what we would do. I realized that back in America Christian people work diligently for their money and through their commitment to missions they give sacrificially. The little rural church where I had been a pastor before arriving on the mission field largely was made up of farmers and factory workers who spend hours at their jobs, often for minimal pay. Yet their love for missions caused them each year to give far more than they really could afford to give.

I observed that $250 would buy this man and his family a television set. We could pick up the car; the tax money would not be mentioned any more. We thus would save almost $12,000 of the Lord's money. But is participating in graft and under-the-table secret payments right? Do we Christians participate in corruption simply because it will save the Lord money? Do we ignore the larger truths of the gospel in order to save $12,000?

On the other hand, would we be right to lose $12,000 which good, Christian people have sacrificially given simply because we do not want to participate in the same graft that everyone else does? Wouldn't the best stewardship of the Lord's money be to simply pay the $250 for a new television set and let it bring blessing to those little children in the tax director's family and at the same time save $12,000?

Dr. Levering Evans, a dear, retired pastor friend from America, visited Saigon several years before this experience. He was present one day as a visitor in an executive committee meeting where a debate raged about whether to participate in a questionable decision that could have saved our budget tens of thousands of dollars. The opportunity had arisen to lease a nice office building for a minimal price by depositing the rent monthly in a bank account in the United States rather than paying in local currency. While this was against the law, it was common practice, because American currency was worth far more than local currency which was constantly being devalued. The debate ended with the decision to stand firm in our adherence to the laws of the land. The old pastor had waited wisely throughout the debate without saying anything. Then, the decision made, he spoke with a deep, resonant voice, "Friends, always remember that where God's honor is at stake, He has the money!"

The outcome of the event with the car was that appealing to the minister of economics did receive a reversal of the ruling. The microbus was brought in without customs charge. But what if this ruling had not been reversed? How would we have reacted then? We had frequent opportunities to make such decisions. One such need for decision occurred in a grave situation which involved life and death.

I returned from work one day and found a shoe box on our dining room table. It was carefully taped and sealed. A letter accompanied it. The letter was handwritten and personal from an American friend who worked for a construction company. The letter informed us that he was leaving the country. He had wrapped a gift and placed it in the shoe box. He believed that someday we might need this object. He advised me to open it right away and then keep it for a difficult time when no doubt I would be glad to have it.

Very carefully I cut through the tape and opened the lid. There, wrapped in tissue paper, was a 38-caliber pistol. Under the pistol were numerous rounds of ammunition. I was horrified to see it. My sole purpose for being in Vietnam was to offer eternal life, not death, to people. We were living in a village that was quite isolated and certainly vulnerable with no police protection. But the last thing I wanted in my home was a gun. My reputation and indeed my security was that everyone throughout the area knew me as a pastor— a missionary. Knowing I had a gun would cast serious suspicion on my purpose in that village. I determined that I would have to get rid of it.

The problem was that if I turned it in, the police surely would suspect me for having the gun. If I threw it away, someone might find it and use it unwisely, or children might pick it up and be killed. I thought about burying it. I simply could not decide the best course of action for the moment.

Until I could find the time and way to get rid of it, I put it in the bottom of a desk drawer, covered it over, and locked it up. Several days went by. I continually thought about the best way to get rid of it. Before I could take any action, a terrible event occurred.

It was about 2 in the morning when the first sound of gunfire awakened my family. It sounded rather far off, so we did not worry about it. With each passing moment the firing drew nearer and grew more intense and louder until it sounded as though it was outside of our door. We sprang from the bed to try to determine what was going on. The wooden shutters in the bedrooms quickly were closed and the children placed on the floor for the night. To the north the red glow of tracer bullets going into the air lit the night sky. I surmised that they were attacking the bridge just up the road from our house. As I looked toward the south to the city of Saigon, I was greatly alarmed. The night sky glowed red with what evidently were many huge fires. Little did I know that the entire country at that moment was under intense attack. This would be one of the bloodiest nights of the entire war.

It was the occasion of the lunar New Year festival commonly known as Tet. Usually a cease-fire was called between opposing forces in order to celebrate the eve and day of the lunar New Year. The communist forces had chosen to take the occasion of the cease-fire to launch the fiercest offensive of the entire war—the infamous "Tet Offensive."

Thousands of troops had moved from the countryside and had concealed themselves in areas around the cities and had waited for this night. Their presence had been perfectly hidden. Little precaution had been taken by either government or American forces. The entire country was vulnerable.

Our village of Thu Duc, 12 kilometers north of Saigon, was on one of the invasion routes into the capital city of Saigon. The firing that we were experiencing was because of the movement of communist forces through the area en masse and meeting the resistance of forces loyal to the government. The military academy where military officers were trained was very near Thu Duc and was under heavy attack. Small bases within our village itself were being attacked. We actually were surrounded by gunfire.

As I moved in the darkness from window to window, I could detect the movement of troops as they passed furtively through our village streets. I had no way of knowing if they were going house to house or whether they would enter our house. My family was on the floor in one of our bedrooms. We were taking every precaution to be quiet and to not attract any attention. I knew that on such occa-

106

sions as this, the opposing forces often gave soldiers medication which caused them to be crazed and unable to act responsibly. The situation was very grave.

As the situation became more ominous, I crawled to my desk, unlocked the drawer, and withdrew the 38-caliber pistol. I carefully loaded it and went back to the front windows. After nearly 30 minutes the firing died down.

As we sat in the quiet of the moment, I looked down at my hands. I was holding the loaded gun ready for use. I had spent a total of six years in the United States Navy. I had been trained to use a gun. During those years that was a part of my life and job.

However, I had determined to commit myself to a different kind of life. I had put down my guns in order to take up the Word of God to give my life to the task of bringing to the world the hope of eternal life. I had a sick feeling in my stomach. I am a man of God serving as a missionary. How could I use a gun to take a life?

If enemy soldiers saw me with a gun, they easily would overwhelm me and kill me and perhaps my family immediately. They would have no idea what I stood for in life and Whom I represented. I would be no different from the hundreds of thousands of other people who live and die by guns and who place their hopes for survival in the power of the gun.

In the quiet of those moments I went back to my desk, put the gun in the shoe box in the drawer, covered it carefully, and locked it up. I made the decision not to use it. During the quiet of those moments I never have felt closer to the Lord. I felt as though He were sitting in the darkness with us. His presence was intimate and precious, as though He was assuring that His will would be done and that everything would be perfect and right in the end.

A few moments later a second wave of attack hit. The firing was even more intense than before. The sky was lit up with flares fired by government troops to reveal the location of the enemy forces. Tracer bullets from all kinds of guns lit up the sky. Again I detected movement outside of our house and yard. I saw one figure dart quickly into the yard next door. In only a matter of time someone likely would be at our house also.

Quickly I returned to my desk, unlocked the drawer, and pulled out the gun. I carefully loaded it and crawled back to my place of surveillance. Then and there I made the decision that if anyone tried to enter our doorway, I would kill. I would not let anyone get to my family. I simply would not sit there and wait for something tragic to happen when I had a means at my disposal to at least attempt to spare my family. For the remainder of those hours of darkness I kept the gun in my hand.

As dawn rose, the sound of helicopters and gunships circled overhead. Bursts of fire were heard continuously as the search was on for concentrations of enemy troops. The news of the events of the night began to be heard over the radio. The entire nation was under attack. Thousands of people had been killed, but war still was raging. Later we heard news that six missionaries in the central highlands had been killed by a squad of North Vietnamese soldiers who had gone boldly into the Christian and Missionary Alliance compound and murdered the six deliberately. An entire Wycliffe missionary family in central Vietnam had been carried away captive.

That night the gunships and helicopters continued to hover overhead. The tracer bullets streaming rapidly down from these guns looked like rivers of hot lava pouring from the black sky. They were firing into our village market place where many enemy forces had gathered and set up a communication center. Our village clearly was in the process of being destroyed.

No more water was available. Electricity was cut off. Leaving the house for food or any kind of assistance was impossible. Fortunately we always kept a supply of food stashed away for such an emergency. For five days this continued until a measure of security was restored.

During that time, the small gun was available. I never had to use it. I do not doubt that I would have used it if necessary. Some will immediately say that any use of that gun would have been disobeying the Lord's commands. Others equally committed to the Lord would say that I would have been foolish not to try to protect my family when I had some means at my disposal. What is right to do under those anguishing circumstances? I made the decision with the best understanding I had and a very acute consciousness of the Lord's presence with me. I always will have to live with my decision, right or wrong.

Three years later I was in the United States doing graduate study at Southeastern Baptist Theological Seminary. I was in a seminar with 10 young graduate students. The discussion was on the Ten Commandments and current issues in Christian ethics. As the discussion turned to war and killing, the students had a consensus that no excuse exists for a Christian to take another person's life. The issue was settled rather quickly and simply based on important principles. I sat there looking into the faces of these young students who had spent their entire lives in the United States of America. Most of them had spent their lives basically in rural or small-town U.S.A. They all were recent high-school and college graduates who had gone directly from college into the seminary. They never had been faced with the horror of warfare descending suddenly on their home in the middle of the night.

Several times I wanted to cry out and say, "Wait! Things are not as simple as that!" But then I thought, how can they understand? Perhaps those who live daily in the ghettos of urban America and daily face the problems of a social order devoid of clean Christian principles can begin to share an understanding. Every Vietnam veteran would know immediately the agony of decisions made in the midst of such an atmosphere and the lingering effects of such decisions. Perhaps the ability to make good decisions under such stress occurs with age. Perhaps this occurs with time. Perhaps this occurs with experience. One thing seems certain; no one can predict how a person will react under extremely stressful circumstances. Having strong personal values based on solid biblical principles certainly helps guide decision-making at any point in life.

Whether we live in the midst of war or enjoy the privilege of a life in a peaceful environment, communicate with the Lord, study His Word on a continuing basis, and adopt a personal value system so that at least you have a basis for thinking through a decision when times are difficult. Whether you are making a decision about a

Volkswagen microbus or the face-to-face encounter with death really doesn't matter. Each is important in its own way. At those moments one's very life and thought can be permeated with a prior knowledge and experience in the Word of God, prayer, and a practice of obedience to the Lord Jesus. In the end one makes a decision with the best light available.

I much rather would make that decision with a full understanding of God's Word and an intimate sense of the Lord's presence than to enter that experience with a shallow familiarity with the Lord Jesus or with a simplistic approach to easily stated principles. Given many people's shallow understanding of the Christian faith, no one is surprised that decisions are made which internally cause so much guilt, shame, and a need for forgiveness and repentance. How tragic that so much of our guilt and shame occurs because we are afraid of what others think of our actions and how they might judge our decisions. Too often we know or care more about the opinions of people than about the mind of Christ.

The peace of mind and heart surpasses all of our understanding when we know that our decision was made with an unmistakable awareness of the very presence of the Lord and the fullness of the Holy Spirit within us. Oh, to live each moment with the Lord in such a way that no decision is made without this precious awareness!

CHAPTER 11

Discussion Questions

This chapter presents two very significant ethical and moral decisions. Is one ethically right to disobey the law in order to gain a more favorable financial position for the Lord's work as a matter of stewardship? Or should one obey the law even though it may mean a less favorable position financially for the Lord?

Is taking another person's life ever acceptable? Do extenuating circumstances blur the lines on this moral decision?

Use the following questions as an opportunity to discuss your own spiritual pilgrimage as a follower of Jesus:

1. In some cultures, the civil-service system pays its workers so little that the only way they can live is to demand money "under the table", even though the law forbids it. This attitude permeates the atmosphere. Does the Christian worker adopt the cultural tradition in order to protect the financial position of his or her organization even if he or she knows it is illegal and wrong?

2. What would you do if your family members were in a highly threatened position and you had the means to protect them, even if this meant taking another person's life and possibly losing your own?

3. What determines the moral and ethical decisions that guide your decision-making process? Does concern about how other people might judge you? Does the Bible? Does culture? Does family teaching? Do you have a value system? Do all of these things guide that decision?

Chapter 12

Love of God and Country

Sometime after midnight, I waked from a deep sleep to hear the doorbell ringing insistently. Still groggy I made my way to the door. For our bell to ring late at night was not unusual. Often an American serviceman would stop by for coffee and a friendly visit. For this to occur at 1 or 2 in the morning, however, was unusual!

At first I did not recognize the tall American who greeted me as I opened the door. Apologizing profusely he hurried past me into the room. I finally recognized him as a frequent attendee at the Trinity Baptist Church in Saigon—a church comprised almost entirely of American servicemen. While I worked with Vietnamese, I often attended the American church when I could. I remembered a missionary remarking that this man had some strange habits. Sometimes he would arrive at church in civilian clothes. Again he would arrive dressed as an army major. One might see him on the streets of Saigon in some other form of dress such as a navy lieutenant commander. No one had taken the opportunity to find out exactly who this man really was. Thus I was more than surprised to find him visiting us when we had no idea who he was.

He suggested that we turn on a small lamp rather than many bright lights so as not to attract too much attention at that hour of the morning. He seemed a bit nervous as I got him a cup of coffee and settled back to discover why he was at our home.

I asked him how he had arrived, since I did not see a vehicle outside and had not heard a taxi on our street. He replied that his Jeep with its driver was parked about two blocks away. He did not want to create problems for us should someone see an army Jeep stop outside our home at that hour of the morning. Dressed as a civilian walking through the neighborhood, he would not attract attention.

I was interested to hear him say what so many other servicemen often said about our home. He said, "I would have been here much sooner had I known that you have such a nice home. I thought missionaries would be living in a thatched-roof hut and eating food that an American could not tolerate. This is really nice."

I thanked him and told him how grateful we are that we could enjoy this kind of house. "We are here for many years. We need to take care of our health and emotional well-being. Thus we try to live as normally as we possibly can within reason and not too far above the people," I said.

"I notice that you do not have a guard outside," he observed. "I thought that all Americans in Vietnam kept a guard outside their gate for protection. Actually, I would feel really vulnerable living with my family exposed like this," he said.

I replied that we are simply missionaries ministering to people and trying to communicate the good news of Jesus Christ to the people of Vietnam. I said, "We have nothing to fear. We try to keep from being caught up in any kind of political involvement. Some would see all Americans as being anti-communists. Actually we try our best to avoid any kind of political stand. We try to be pro-Christ. We believe that if people can know Jesus Christ, He will transform their lives in such a way that needed changes will occur."

"That sounds good, but I wonder if it is practical," he said. I poured another cup of coffee and asked if he would like to spend the night with us. "No," he replied. "I really appreciate the invitation. Maybe I can take you up on it later. I need to get to the reason for my visit."

He began slowly and deliberately. "As you must know, many of our officers quarters and bachelor-enlisted quarters have been blown up by communist guerrillas over the past months. A part of my assignment is to try to determine where guerrillas are situated and to try to destroy their infrastructure. We have reason to believe that a cell of these men operates within a four- to five-block radius of your house right here. We believe that they are responsible for blowing up several of our officer and enlisted quarters. I'm here to ask a favor of you."

I was feeling very uncomfortable at the turn of the conversation. I remained silent and listened.

He continued, "I understand that you speak Vietnamese fluently and are well-acquainted with the people in this neighborhood. I believe that if you watch carefully, you may be able to see anything unusual. I will be glad to train you some and help you to understand what we try to spot. For example, any gathering of young men or people you would consider strange in the neighborhood might indicate the presence of this cell. We need some continuing eyes and ears here to carefully observe everything that goes on. We want to know everything that might give us a clue to their location." With that he stopped and waited for my reply.

Seldom had I been filled with so many mixed emotions. A feeling of patriotism welled up within me. This was something I could do for my country. My sense of pride at being a six-year navy veteran and once again being used by my country stirred excitement within me. I wanted to immediately say, "Yes, let's go for it!"

My mind raced back over the events of the past months. Recently Rachel and I had been walking in downtown Saigon and heard a tremendous explosion. We determined the exact direction and rushed to the scene just a block away. The United States Embassy had been blown up. Everyone in the area appeared injured. Within moments ambulances and military personnel flooded the area.

Dozens of people emerged bloody and dazed. No question—this was a serious attack. We realized the magnitude of the injuries and that Rachel as a highly trained registered nurse might help.

Rachel went immediately to the naval hospital to volunteer. She began working as special nurse for some of the more critically injured female employees of the embassy. For long hours she worked in that environment. Seeing the tragedy of war so close to us was an emotional experience. Some said that they had heard shots in the street below the embassy. They went to the window to see. At that very moment a car loaded with explosives was detonated. The glass from the windows imploded into the rooms. The faces and in some cases the eyes of those who looked out were cut. Some

114

of the secretaries had been blinded by these injuries. We both were moved deeply to see our fellow Americans suffer so.

The Christmas before this I had preached in a large Chinese church in Cholon, the Chinese section of Saigon. On the way home I had just slowed for traffic when a huge explosion occurred. A huge piece of the concrete wall hit my right front wheel. This caused me to veer partially onto the sidewalk. I sat there stunned by the force of the explosion. I suddenly realized that my nose was bleeding from the concussion of the blast. Just across the street a bar had been blown up. Numerous American servicemen were staggering out of the bar stunned and confused by the force of the blast. The entire front wall had been obliterated. Inside the mangled bodies of bar servers and several servicemen were strewn across the debris-littered floor. Again, seeing my own fellow countrymen lying dead and injured was an emotional experience.

Occasionally a young serviceman would visit our home in the evening for a cup of coffee and some fellowship. As the hour grew late, we would invite him to stay for the night. Very quickly he accepted the invitation. On most of these occasions that serviceman would have had a premonition that his quarters would be blown up or that some other tragedy would strike. Visiting the missionary's house and spending the night seemed safer. We always were pleased that they felt free to do that. But it reminded us of how close the war was to all of us, especially to these young men.

Thus my first impression was to do everything that I could to prevent these kinds of bombings. However, I also was in touch with other feelings that welled up within me. Up to now I always had the security of knowing that the only reason for our being in Vietnam was to share the gospel of our Lord. I already had spent six years of my life in the U.S. Navy. Three of these were in the Korean War. I had given up my weapons of war to bring the Prince of Peace to the peoples of the world. We had refrained from involvement in any kind of political maneuverings. Our contacts with American military were mostly in response to them and were limited. We avoided becoming identified strongly with American military or government. With a clear conscience I lived with the Vietnamese people as a missionary without political involvement in the war effort. I was exactly who I said I was—a missionary under the Great Commission of our Lord to share the gospel.

From time to time rumors would be heard that this missionary or that one was affiliated with the C.I.A. or some other intelligence-gathering operation. Making absolutely sure that everyone in our community and neighborhood knew us well and knew us as persons belonging only to Jesus Christ was important to me. For this reason we could live without guards and feel reasonably secure.

I realized that the moment I began to use my Vietnamese language and my knowledge of the people for something other than what had motivated me, I would have embarked on a new kind of life. Never again would I be able to say that my sole commitment is to Jesus Christ and His mission in Vietnam. Never again would I feel safe, because I always would wonder if anyone out there knew that I am doing something that I cannot reveal or share openly. The need for information in a place like Vietnam is staggering. If I embarked on this course for this one exercise, I easily could be called on again for another problem just as acute.

After some moments of thought I shared with the man why I could not respond affirmatively to his request. I wanted him to know that when he arrived at my home, the fact that he did not see a guard at my gate was important to me. This says to every Vietnamese that the American who lives here has nothing to fear and nothing to hide. I can feel perfectly secure, because I have done nothing to cause anyone to want to take my life.

I shared with him that six years of my life had been spent serving my country before, during, and after the Korean War. I am proud beyond description that I am a veteran of that war and that I gave the best that I had to offer to my country for that time.

I tried to help him understand the nature and character of a sacred call of God to serve Him. I never will know why God chose me and placed me in Vietnam at this crucial juncture in history. He did choose me; I yielded to Him. I gave myself to acquire years of education and training in order to become the very best missionary that I can be. I also have returned to the Lord who created them my hands, feet, voice, and total being absolutely yielded for His use. Every gift and talent that I have, the Lord gave to me. They are His completely, totally, and no longer mine to determine their use. If I am to serve the Lord as a missionary, I will have to do it with all of my heart, mind, soul, and strength. To dilute it with other commitments would not be possible.

Above all I tried to share with him that I honor his commitment to the task he has been given to do in the military. Some of the greatest men of God that I have ever met were the military chaplains in Vietnam. Some of the most dedicated Christians I have ever known were among the servicemen we knew during those years in Vietnam. I wanted him to know that I am persuaded that every military person in Vietnam deserves every bit of the respect and love that we can give. Their sacrifice is great. I must honor the fact that they are doing what is right for them to do. I also must ask him to honor that to which I have committed my life.

Seeing the reaction of this man was good. On learning of my decision he responded with great respect and diplomacy. He seemed to understand completely and apologized for troubling me with this and placing me in such a difficult position. He excused himself and disappeared into the night.

To become a missionary and go overseas does not mean that one loves his own country less. Sometimes when we were privileged to return to America on Stateside assignments and saw the flag wave proudly after such a long absence, we shed tears. The question remains as to how much one mixes patriotism and love of country with absolute commitment to the Lord and His service. This was the question I faced that night. No doubt I still struggle with it. Had I made the decision emotionally, I would have done everything I could to respond to my patriotic nature and to locate that cell of guerrillas. Perhaps this would have saved the lives of some of my countrymen. Other forces intervened to help me to see the other aspects of my unique call of God and to prevent me from veering away from the call and purpose which brought me to Vietnam.

Another principle always has been important to me. I've always believed that the Christian ought to live his or her life so that anything in that person's life could be revealed. Transparency is of utmost importance to one who would serve God. No greater peace exists than to live one's life without fear of someone finding out something secret. That next morning I felt good going out into my neighborhood and hearing people say, in all sincerity, "Good morning, pastor." I felt even better being able to receive that greeting with all sincerity and integrity.

CHAPTER 12

Discussion Questions

This chapter presents a significant dilemma: Does patriotism have priority over all other loyalties, or does patriotism have a rightful place among all other loyalties depending on circumstances?

In view of the chapter you just read, use the following questions to discuss your own spiritual pilgrimage as a follower of Jesus:

1. Given similar circumstances what would be your response to the request to become involved in information or intelligence gathering in order to save your countrymen?

2. Can you cite a circumstance in which loyalty to one's country commands an equal priority with loyalty to Christ?

3. When you live in a culture that differs from your own, how do you deal with the sensitive issue of fellowshiping, influencing and being influenced by your own culture people living in that different culture with you, and fellowshiping, influencing, and being influenced by the local, national people to whom you have been called to serve? How do you balance your time in these two arenas?

Chapter 13

Half a House

The choir already had lined up to enter the auditorium. The congregation was seated; everything was ready for the morning worship service to begin. I stood near the front door of the church outside in a little patio which served as a reception area for people before they entered the building. I often stood there greeting people until the service began.

Just as I turned to enter the auditorium, a woman with a little girl about 5 ran toward me calling, "Pastor, pastor!" I stopped and turned toward her. Breathless from running, she paused for a moment to catch her breath and to regain her composure. Then she said, "This is my daughter. I want to give her to you, pastor." With that she took the little girl's hand and placed it in mine. I looked down into one of the most beautiful little faces I had seen. Her large, brown, almond-shaped eyes with long eyelashes were captivating. When I looked at her, she instantly smiled as though she were saying, "I like you. I want to live with you!"

I stood on the steps of Grace Church. The entire congregation was seated and waited for me to enter the church. The choir was restless and awaited my signal to file in. I was speechless. I looked at the woman, then at the child, then at the church. I looked back at the woman and saw the mournful face of a middle-aged woman. Her facial lines and bent shoulders suggested an age far beyond her actual years. She had a harried look about her. Her whole bearing suggested anxiety, frustration, and a difficult life. Her dress was clean and neat but evidently well-worn. The little girl was clean with clothes neatly pressed. Much about their appearance said that they were not from among the hundreds of beggars or street people who often were ready to give away a child for money. This woman was different and compelled my attention. As I looked at her, I was

119

filled with compassion. I knelt and hugged the little girl. I felt fear and tension lift as she lifted those big brown eyes and looked deep into my own eyes.

I quickly stood and said to the mother, "Please be seated in the church. I will talk with you after the worship service." She readily agreed and entered the church.

As I sat at the podium, I could not help but look at this strange woman and her little daughter. I had worked diligently on my sermon for that Sunday. Now, this sermon did not seem appropriate any longer. I began to pray desperately for the Lord to guide me toward what I should say. I preached about the compassionate Christ whose love not only changes us but enables us to rise above our circumstances in life and to be victorious in our living.

As was the custom at the close of the sermon an invitation was given to anyone in the congregation to publicly receive Christ as Savior or to share a decision the person might have made as a result of their worship. To my amazement this mother walked down the aisle and led her daughter by the hand.

She said to me, "All of my life I have searched for this kind of love and compassion. I knew that it could be found somewhere, but I never have experienced it before. I want to believe in this Jesus you have just told us about. I want to know more about Him. I think He can help us. Would you visit our home and teach my family and neighbors what you have just shared with us this morning?"

Again I was almost speechless. I suggested that we have prayer together and talk more about this after the church dismissed.

When everyone left, I sat on the front pew of the church with the woman and her daughter and talked with her about the seriousness of her decision. I explained fully the meaning of her decision and what it meant in the future. She seemed almost ecstatic as she accepted Christ as her Savior. The more I shared with her, the more excited she became. Not once did she mention giving her daughter to us.

I asked, "Where do you live?" She replied, "In a small alleyway just off Petrusky Street. You know where all of the buses travel to and from over the country?" She wrote the address on a piece of paper. Her name was Mrs. Chieu; her daughter's name was Be. I was so excited at the possibilities this offered, I could hardly contain myself.

Petrusky Street long had been the focus of our attention. We had conducted numerous surveys to see where to start new churches. At the top of the list was this area of the city. Our major problem was that we had no connections there. None of our national Christians lived there. Our Christians had no relatives in this part of town. Knowing how to gain entry into the homes and to find a place to meet would be a problem.

Our strategy for Saigon called for churches to begin as home Bible studies which would be reproducible. This was preferable to renting buildings at great expense and then being locked into that location for a long period of time whether the response was good or not. Dependency on a building had a chilling effect on the rapid reproduction of the church. The church seemed to settle into the building and wait for people to visit to receive Christ. Having a building saddled the church with not only the constant expense of upkeep but the purchase price itself. Thus wherever we started a church, having someone in the area who willingly would open his or her home for a Bible study was necessary. Such a place was not always easy to find, especially in poor places where houses were little more than temporary shacks and very small.

The Petrusky Street area was an exciting area. About five blocks of this street served as something like a bus station. Buses parked on the street. No bus terminal or station as such existed. Bus drivers wrote the time of departure and destination on the windshield and back windows of the bus. People would walk along the street until they found a bus going to their destination. They then bought their ticket either from the driver or a young assistant who traveled with him on the bus to help the driver with menial chores. They would wait for either the time for departure as published or for the bus to fill with passengers, at which time it would leave regardless of the published hour. Engines, transmissions, and other parts of buses usually were scattered all over the street as repairs were made in preparation for their next trip. Hawkers arrived from all over town with their wares. Children went from bus to bus selling small plastic bags of sweet sugar cane cut into small round pieces. Fruit vendors were everywhere. Newspaper boys mingled with the people and begged them to buy their papers. Early in the morning about six the noise was deafening as buses started their engines, hawkers called out their goods, passengers bought food and fruit for their journeys, and young men loaded baggage onto the top of the buses and tied the bags down securely.

One of the emotional parts of visiting this scene was the evidence of the war. Soldiers with missing limbs begged on the street among the people. Soldiers constantly were arriving from battlefields hoping for a brief visit home before returning. Young women stopped soldiers as they got off of the bus asking what unit they were with and if they knew their husbands. One day I heard a shrill cry of anguish. When I inquired what happened, I learned that a young woman had asked an arriving soldier about her husband. He told her that a few days before, he was with her husband when he was killed and had helped to bury him. Happy moments also occurred, when wives, mothers, or girlfriends met their men returning from the countryside. I sometimes referred to that street as a "street of tears"—tears of sorrow, sometimes tears of joy. The place was vibrant with life.

In this vicinity I had hoped a new church could begin. Off this street behind the storefronts ran small alleyways clogged with houses and thousands of people. If only a church could be established among these thousands of people with their raw, naked hurt and anguish as they traveled all over the country! The good news of Christ and all He represents could be carried from that place to the uttermost parts of the nation.

The sudden appearance of Mrs. Chieu and her daughter and her commitment of her life to the Lord now would make a significant ministry in this area possible.

We returned home from church that day thrilled at Mrs. Chieu's profession of faith. About four that afternoon our doorbell rang incessantly. Looking out the window we saw Mr. and Mrs. Chieu standing at the gate. He looked uncomfortable and impatient as he rang the bell. With considerable anxiety Rachel and I invited them into the house. Mr. Chieu's first question was, "What have you done to my wife?" The question seemed ominous. Did he not want his wife to become a Christian? Before either of us could answer, he continued, "She has made a dramatic change. She is different. I want to know what makes this difference."

We looked at Mrs. Chieu to see how she was reacting to this. Her face was beaming with a beautiful smile. Somehow we knew that everything would be all right. We immediately began to share with him about Jesus who had changed his wife so dramatically. Mr. Chieu could hardly take it in fast enough. He said, "Anything that can make that kind of change in my wife is something that I also need." He gloriously accepted Christ as his Savior. His first words were, "Please visit our home and share this with all of our neighbors. We will get them all together if you will visit." I immediately offered to do this the following evening.

Rachel and I arrived at the Chieu house a few minutes before seven. We had to park our van on the street and make our way through the maze of narrow alleys to the house. We were surprised to find 14 people crowded into a small room about 20-feet long by 12-feet wide. I never had seen a village of houses built like this.

The walls of each of these houses were made of sheets of beer-can tins. Some were sheets of metal, printed with beer labels, and ready to be cut out and formed into beer cans. Others had taken all kinds of cans—beer and soft drinks—cut the top and bottom off, and flattened the tin. Each of the flattened sheets was welded together to others to form a large sheet. These sheets of metal then were nailed to supporting posts to form walls for the houses. A door then was set into the front wall for entry. No windows existed. Thatched straw and sheets of tin formed the roof.

Inside, the house was divided into two rooms—a living room and a back room which served as kitchen and storage area. The front room was about 12-feet wide and 20-feet long. The kitchen area was about 12-feet wide and six-feet deep. A small ladder in the living room led upward to a loft which extended over the kitchen area. The two larger children slept in the loft. All of the adults slept in the front room.

The two rooms were divided by pieces of pasteboard boxes cut into strips and nailed to wooden supports. In the front room was a wide, wooden surface on which the husband, wife, their smallest child, and the elderly grandmother slept. The floor was made of hard-pressed earth and swept clean with a broom. A single light bulb swung from the center of the front-room ceiling. This provided the only light in the room. All down the alleyway each house shared a common tin wall with the house next to it, so that each house basically leaned against the house beside it and was inseparable from it.

I soon discovered that almost all of the houses in this area were built in a similar fashion. The people living here were basically "squatters" who had moved into Saigon from many locations, found work, and pieced together their houses from whatever sources they could find.

As we entered the house every available space was taken. We were given the only two stools in the room. Others had brought stools from their own houses or sat on the clean, dirt floor. We began by getting acquainted with those who were present. All were neighbors of the Chieu family. I learned that Mrs. Chieu's husband was a sailor on board a merchant ship that plied the coastal waters of Vietnam. He seldom was at home. However, Mr. Chieu was present for this first service. Mrs. Chieu's grandmother was 90 years old. She was a diminutive woman with a slight stoop. She had only one or two teeth. Her head was completely shaved. She insisted on staying outside the house behind the kitchen in the alleyway. She was a devout Buddhist and was in total disagreement with her daughter and son-in-law embracing a "new religion." She was very unfriendly and opposed to our teaching the Bible in their home.

Also in the group gathered that first night was the Duc family who lived next door. Their house shared a common wall with the Chieu family. Mr. and Mrs. Duc had four children. Their house was the identical size of Mr. and Mrs. Chieu's house. A variety of other neighbors also were present.

During the course of the evening Mr. Duc asked many significant questions. He was a common laborer but evidently was highly intelligent. On the second night of meetings he and his wife accepted Jesus as Savior and immediately joined in discipleship courses along with Mr. and Mrs. Chieu. After two weeks of meeting, five new Christians formed the nucleus of this new "house church."

On the second evening of teaching at the Chieu home, the elderly grandmother moved her stool from the alleyway behind the kitchen into the kitchen itself. Within a month she sat beside the doorway leading from the kitchen into the front room. She had her hand cupped to her ear so that she could hear better. Within another two weeks she had moved her stool next to my wife. After six months she asked if she could accept Jesus as her Savior and be baptized. What a day it was when this 90-year-old grandmother followed the Lord in baptism at Grace Church! When she emerged from out of the water, her face broke into the most beautiful smile I ever have seen.

During one of the evenings as we discipled those who had believed, Mrs. Chieu began to talk intimately about her family. I never had asked her about her daughter and whether she still wanted to give her away. She had not mentioned it again to me since she became a Christian. She told how her merchant-seaman husband would come home once or twice a month when his ship was in. Before he became a Christian, he would make one of his rare appearances at home and entered the house drunk, cursing and terrifying everyone.

On several occasions he had beaten their daughter, Be, severely. We learned that little Be was the daughter of her former husband, who was a Frenchman. This meant that Be was one of those highly despised, "mixed-blood" children who always would be considered second-class citizens in the Vietnamese society. Usually when he arrived home drunk, reasoning with him was difficult. He seemed to delight in taking his anger out on their little girl. Mrs. Chieu began fearing that he might kill their daughter. After one of those experiences she began to try to find a way to get their daughter to a safe place. A relative living in another part of town was knowledgeable about Grace Church and provided the name and address of the church. She also found out that the pastor was an American missionary and often helped people who were in trouble. On that recommendation she had brought her daughter on that Sunday morning to meet me at Grace Church.

Never in her life had she been in a Christian church. She was more familiar with Catholics but never had attended a Catholic church. She told how fearful she was as she approached me that Sunday. She had not intended to attend the church but to leave the little girl in safe hands. In fact, she wanted to leave the little girl and not provide any address at all. When I suggested that she sit in the church and talk after the service, she said that she felt a strange compulsion to do that. She could not adequately describe her joy and relief when she heard about the hope we have in Christ Jesus. This changed all of her plans.

She saw that by having Christ in her heart, she could have forgiveness for the terrible life she had lived with her French lover. She could overcome the terrible situation she now was in.

She also held out hope that her husband could know Christ and would not continue to terrorize their family. No small wonder she was overjoyed when her husband wanted to receive Christ!

After several months of meeting, a strange event occurred. Fire broke out in that little community. In a poor community such as this the most dreaded thing that can happen is fire. No fire-fighting service is available. Little water is available. In houses made of pasteboard and old scrap lumber the fire spreads quickly from house to house. It often ignites kerosene containers and explodes. This further spreads the flames. The night this fire began, it moved rapidly down several of the small streets and alleyways. It gradually burned every home on the street where the Chieu family lived until it reached their house. It burned the house next door. It charred the common wall between their house and the house next door which was destroyed. It did not burn through the wall or burn the roof of the Chieu house. It also did not touch Mr. Duc's house, which shared the opposite wall with the Chieus. While dozens of homes were destroyed, the Chieus' home was spared, as was the home of Mr. Duc and all the homes down the remainder of the alley.

When I arrived, I was horrified to see the damage to the little community. I was not certain what the peoples' attitude would be.

126

Some Vietnamese, like Americans and others, hold superstitious beliefs. That afternoon as I visited the people up and down the streets, they seemed to have a respect and reverence I had not experienced before. A woman soothsayer began telling the villagers that the Chieu and the Duc homes had been spared because of the tall man of God who teaches the Bible in their home. An immediate upsurge of attendance completely crowded out the little meeting room in their house and spilled over into the alleyway.

I often wondered what would have happened had their house burned. This could have been a sign of the disapproval of spirits because the community was allowing this Christian religion to be taught there! Two years later I found out what probably would have happened. On the Saigon River just north of the city was a small fishing village that never had a Christian witness of any kind. I took several seminary students there to begin visiting and ministering in that village. Within a brief time a large group of people gathered every Sunday afternoon. Within weeks I had turned the group over to one of my seminary students to serve as pastor.

The oldest person in the village, along with several others, accepted Christ. When Christmas arrived, the little church planned its first Christmas celebration. Members organized a parade to walk through the main streets of the village on Christmas Eve. They made a huge star out of paper and placed a candle in the center. They fastened it to a pole. This star lifted high above the village. Carried by the pastor it would lead the parade through the village. About halfway through the village a strong gust of wind blew the candle over and ignited the paper star. It blazed high into the night.

Many villagers took this as a bad omen. Two days after Christmas the oldest villager who had been one of the first in the village to become a Christian was taken ill. By January 1 he was dead. The villagers passed the word that the burning star signaled death and destruction. This house church would have to leave and never return. The young pastor was cast out of the village. This was a great burden to all of the seminary students. We were completely helpless to correct the situation in face of the strong folk beliefs of these fishermen.

This could have been a disaster in the Chieus' community had their home burned. The fact that the home of the Christian leaders did not burn led to the rapid growth of the little church there.

As the weeks went by, Mr. Chieu began returning home more frequently. He did not want to miss a Bible study. He and his next-door neighbor became the strong leadership of the house church. Under their leadership the house church grew in numbers and in faith. Often American servicemen would ask to go with me to one of my Bible studies. They enjoyed going to the Chieu home. They could not understand the language but sensed the warm, Christian fellowship that had developed there. They often asked permission to take pictures of the Bible-study group. One night as one of the servicemen showed me his slides, I was amused to see a picture of me teaching the Bible with the wall behind me made of Budweiser and Pabst Blue Ribbon beer cans. Those names were prominent in every slide! I wondered what church people in America would think when he showed them those pictures of one of their missionaries!

Teaching everyone who wanted to attend the services was increasingly impossible. The little space was completely crowded out, with many people sitting in the alleyway outside. Something needed to be done. Our method of starting churches was to let the Christians provide their own meeting space. We did everything we could to prevent churches from depending on foreign sources for their income and for the maintenance of their church. Never once did I mention larger facilities or offer them money to provide more space. I often suggested that we find other houses in which we could open new "house churches." I taught the Bible faithfully. That included the concept of stewardship. These were very poor people, but they would want to share their meager resources with the Lord.

One night Mr. Chieu and Mr. Duc, deeply concerned for their church, visited me. They said that their church could not grow any more until a larger meeting place could be found. They did not want to divide the congregation by starting another house church. They said the people now attending were joined in a holy body. To divide it would not be good. They also said that no quiet place existed where they could bring their friends to talk with them and to pray.

They were concerned that the church had no place for the children to learn about the Bible. They asked that we covenant together to pray for the Lord's leadership in providing what they called a "holy place." The entire group began to pray earnestly.

The next Sunday they suggested that we set aside a part of the offering each Sunday for a place to meet. They hoped that this would help both with the church expenses and provide a new facility. Several months passed. They were accruing some funds, but a long time would be necessary before enough could be gathered to rent a new space. Mr. Duc and Mr. Chieu asked for some personal time with me to talk this over. I supposed that they might ask for a loan or for a grant to provide the facilities. This was not so.

Mr. Chieu started the conversation by pointing out that their house church had used the living room of his home now for many months. The Chieus had been grateful that they could provide this space. However, their living room was much too small and afforded no privacy for the church. He informed me that Mr. Duc and he had consulted together and had made a decision.

These two families shared a common wall about 20-feet long. They proposed cutting their common wall out about 10 feet. This would open the wall between their two living rooms. They then would build a wall across their two houses so that a large worship space would be in front of both their houses about 10-feet deep and nearly 24-feet wide. This meant that their families would live in the back part of the house behind the worship room. They would be cutting their houses almost exactly in half in order to provide space for Bible study and worship for the community.

I said to them, "Do you realize what you are proposing? This means, Mr. Duc, that you, your wife, and your four children will be living in a space about 10-feet long and 12-feet wide. Mr. Chieu, you, your wife, your three children, and your grandmother will live in a space the same size. I am not sure that is possible. You are giving half of your house to the Lord!"

I never shall forget the expressions on their faces as they looked straight into my eyes and replied, "But, Pastor, Jesus gave His all for us. The least we can do is to give him half of our house."

Later, God provided facilities in a different location, in a different way. However, never has a church building been any more beautiful than this one in a living room with a dirt floor, tin walls made of beer cans, and a thatched roof, with two men who saw that having Jesus is far more to be desired than houses and lands and the abundance of things possessed.

CHAPTER 13

Discussion Questions

This chapter presents a very interesting dilemma: When the need for a special place to worship, such as a church building, is so great, should people outside of the church family be asked to provide the funds, or should the church family provide for its own place of worship without depending on outside funds?

In view of the chapter you just read, use the following questions as an opportunity to discuss your own pilgrimage as a follower of Jesus:

1. Should the missionary in this case appeal to more wealthy people in America and other countries to help provide this house church with funds for their place to worship? If not, why not?

2. What would be the advantages of a strategy to lead this house church to reproduce itself in several different locations which would avoid the necessity of providing a special building? Do you see any disadvantages?

3. Did the sacrifice of these two families seem to increase their love and commitment to the Lord, or did it make them question the lack of outside help to provide a better facility?

Chapter 14

Growing Through Personal Crisis

Serving the Lord in a country at war carries with it the potential for intense family stress but also opportunities for family spiritual growth and closeness. With each crisis event the Lord seemed to draw us closer together as a family and closer to Himself.

This was seen most clearly during the 1968 communist offensive commonly called the "Tet Offensive." On the first night of that massive invasion of communist forces throughout South Vietnam six missionaries in the central highlands were killed deliberately by North Vietnamese troops. The village where we lived just north of Saigon was overrun by communist forces. The fighting began around two in the morning with an attack on a bridge on the main road leading from the huge Long Binh army base and Saigon. Our house was right alongside the highway about 100 yards off of the road in a small housing area called (in English) University Village. Our city of Thu Duc was effectively taken by the communist forces and held for five days and nights. We stayed inside our house out of concern that one or more enemy troops would see our American presence and enter our home. We were without food except for what we kept on hand for such emergencies. Fortunately we lived diagonally from the village water tower. Since our house sat on a slight decline from the water tower, a trickle of water drained into our water pipes. Several times a day we could get a small pot of water for our family use. We had no electricity to run refrigerator, fans, or other appliances. We had no telephone.

Several dead bodies in the vicinity of our house were decomposing in the 100-degree heat. I feared that our children would have an enduring emotional reaction when finally we could leave our house and they would see the devastation and death all about us. An American neighbor who worked for an engineering company lived a couple of blocks from our home. On the first day of this siege he ventured out to visit us. He was inclined to drink alcohol and arrived slightly intoxicated carrying a beer can concealed in one of his socks. When I questioned him about his sock, he replied that he knew I was a missionary. He did not want just to walk in crassly carrying a beer can in his hands!

He explained that the reason for his visit was to invite us to stay at his house. He had a good supply of guns, ammunition, and even a grenade launcher. If our two families were together, he reasoned, we could defend ourselves better. I could just see taking our four children into that house with all of his weapons arsenal and depending on an intoxicated man to lead us in the defense of our families. I thanked him profusely and politely declined. I told him I would rather take my chances in my own home!

During the day air force jets dove right over our house. We could see the bombs released and watch them falling, twisting, and turning into areas at times less than a quarter of a mile from our house. The immediate explosions were deafening. At night helicopters flew in small circles almost directly overhead. They poured fire into the village market and other concentrations of communist forces. Since every third bullet was a tracer bullet, seeing what looked like burning lava pouring out of heaven was impressive. Thoughts of what was happening when those bullets hit the ground were deeply troubling. Many of those in the village were our friends and no doubt would be caught in the devastation of this fighting.

Those days and nights with our family together, sitting around a dim candle, playing games, telling stories, and finding other ways to amuse ourselves became a source of great blessing. Founding a new seminary, getting buildings renovated and facilities equipped, and at the same time teaching a heavy schedule had not allowed much time to be with family. Using seminary students I was starting new churches wherever I could. This took me from home most evenings and all day on Sundays. While being essentially prisoners in our own home held its anxious moments, the blessing of laughing, playing, and praying together during these tense hours was an opportunity we forever would treasure as a family.

During this particular event I learned that children tend to take the attitude of parents to an extreme. If we were afraid, our children were terrified. If we were at peace, our children would go to sleep. I observed this from many perspectives. I saw that if we like our Vietnamese people, our children absolutely loved them. If we spoke disparagingly and disliked the people, our children would hate them. If we liked our fellow missionary families, then our children loved these families and wanted to be around them. As our own history has shown, we love the Lord. Our children not only love the Lord but have all given their lives to serve him—two as missionaries overseas! The attitude of parents has a tremendous long-term effect on children. The five days in Thu Duc with hostile forces all around formed a great laboratory to test this philosophy!

Other times of tension resulted in great personal growth. Once Rachel made a trip to the mountain city of Dalat, a flight of about an hour and a half in an old DC-3 propeller passenger plane belonging to Air Vietnam. I went to the airport around 6 p.m. to wait for her return. About an hour beyond time for her arrival, I asked a young woman about the plane. She simply said, "It is delayed."

Another hour went by. I again asked about the plane. She repeated that the plane was delayed. At around 8:30 p.m., many of the people waiting for the plane were beginning to get anxious and restless. They were asking for answers and getting little or no response. I went to the Air Vietnam office and basically demanded to know about the plane.

The manager of the office replied, "This plane is missing. We have no idea where it is. We do not want to panic the people who are waiting." He said, "For some reason our communications with the airport in Dalat and with the plane have broken down. We cannot contact anyone." Seldom have I experienced such personal anguish. My beloved wife and mother of our children basically was missing. I could not bring myself to share this with the anxious people waiting outside. I asked permission to stay in his office which he gladly granted me this privilege

Ten p.m. arrived. The plane was four hours overdue. During those days we had no telephone to call home and check on the children, who were in the care of a young Vietnamese girl. Yet, I could not bring myself to leave the airport.

I made my way out of the terminal to a quiet spot under some trees in the front of the terminal. I knelt and prayed as earnestly as I ever had prayed. My mind constantly wandered to what I would do if Rachel were killed and I were left with small children. I made my way back to the office and waited.

Around 11:30 we heard a plane land. The manager spoke to someone and ran back elated. He told me that the plane from Dalat had just arrived safely. The plane had a flat tire in Dalat; no tires were available to replace it. They had waited for a tire to be brought to Dalat by truck from the coast, changed the tire, and then flew back to Saigon. This experience, as difficult as it was, in the years ahead brought about a sense of urgency in our love for each other and for our children. Seldom had I felt such tremendous, overwhelming love for my wife!

One afternoon our two boys, one 9 and the other 10 years old, played in the front yard. When we checked on them, they were nowhere to be found. Since the war always was close to us there in the village of Thu Duc, we immediately began to panic. They had been instructed never to leave our yard under any conditions. They knew the seriousness of stepping on a land mine, or getting caught in cross fire, or even getting kidnapped for ransom. Throughout the village I ran, as I frantically looked and called for them. Finally I returned home to see if they might be there.

Rachel and I stood on our porch nearly in tears wondering what to do when we heard the roar of engines. We looked and saw a column of Vietnamese army tanks proceeding slowly up the street in front of our house. Our anxiety heightened; we knew that their approach may represent something horrible about to happen. Just as the second tank reached our house, the column stopped. The top of the tank opened. Out crawled two little blond heads. They were laughing and talking with excitement with the Vietnamese soldiers. About 30 minutes before, this tank had passed by our house on a training mission. We had not seen it pass by. One of the soldiers had invited our two boys to get in the tank and promised to let them drive. That was a temptation no 9- and 10-year-old boy could dismiss! The tank had moved down the road out of the village, formed a column with other tanks, and brought our boys back to our house. Our emotions moved quickly from anxiety, to panic, to fear, and now to white-hot anger, both at the soldiers and our two boys. I normally did not believe in spanking children, but this pushed the limits of my value system! At the same time, never had my great love for these two boys been so sensitive and expressive.

Not many places existed to which one could go to get away from the threat presented by the war. Occasionally our family went to the coastal city of Nhatrang for a few days on the beautiful beaches there. On one such occasion Rachel went into the center of town to a beauty shop. I went to the beach to read and enjoy the quiet. I noticed a Vietnamese air-force plane passing very low over the beach. Just as it was about a mile over the ocean, the two pilots bailed out of the plane. I knew that this kind of plane carries only two pilots. Just as they jumped, the plane lowered its right wing and began to circle. With each circle over the city and back over the beach the plane was significantly lower. Finally I watched in horror as the plane nosed into the very center of the city of Nhatrang. I heard a huge explosion and saw a ball of fire. Immediately I remembered that Rachel was there in the center of the city at this very moment getting her hair fixed. I ran in panic toward town as fast as I could. Just up ahead I saw her walking toward me. I practically fell to my knees in praise to the Lord. I was overwhelmed with joy and grief at the same time.

Rachel had just left the beauty parlor less than 10 minutes before the plane hit. It missed the beauty parlor by several feet. It hit the street in front of the main theater. Its impact carried it through the front doors and inside the theater. A 500-pound bomb exploded. Numerous people were killed or missing. The beauty parlor was totally demolished and everyone inside killed. Once again, life for our family took on a sense of thanksgiving and commitment to each other and to the Lord. We sensed a new urgency about expressing our love for each other and for living our life as fully as possible for the rest of our days on earth. Family became more precious than ever before. Serving the Lord and committing ourselves to Him became the passion of our lives.

I firmly believe that God has something to teach us through every experience, no matter how traumatic it is. We only learn what He has to teach when we bring the experience into the light of His Word and His presence and listen to what He is saying to us.

CHAPTER 14

Discussion Questions

In this chapter is a unique kind of dilemma. Living in the midst of war year in and year out presents a plethora of human need and need for the gospel. It presents numerous opportunities for service and bringing people to know Jesus. Life becomes unbelievably meaningful in the midst of ministry. However, life in the midst of war brings with it anxieties and fears that easily can cripple one's effectiveness. The temptation to run away is great, while an awareness of the benefit of staying is also great. To stay or to leave always is the question.

Use the following questions as an opportunity to explore your own pilgrimage as a follower of Jesus:

1. From your reading of this chapter what are some of the primary benefits of living through various crises as a family?

2. Numerous "what-if's" permeate this chapter. What are some of the "what-if?" times in your own life? How did they affect you and your family?

3. Have you ever processed the difficult personal experiences to see what you learned from them and how they are affecting your life today?

Chapter 15

Preparing for the Future

In January, 1975, I was to go to several sites where students in the various branches of our seminary's theological-education extension program were located. At that time the seminary had about 35 resident students and more than 125 extension students scattered throughout the country. Our methodology was to give the students self-instructional materials to study. Then every few weeks I would visit various locations that had concentrations of students and meet with them to discuss what they were learning. The major requirement for entry into the seminary was that a student had to be actively planting a church or helping to plant a church. Having them study in extension classes kept them in their natural location where they could be in their own cultural context and thus most effective. This was preferable to uprooting them from their own context and bringing them into a strange city to live, study, and minister.

I was to meet about 15 students at Hope Baptist Church in Danang to teach two courses. When I arrived at the church, more than 100 people were seated in the church auditorium. I asked what was going on in the church. They replied that all of these people were there to study the two courses. I was amazed and went in to teach. This particular course was designed to help the church leader know how to minister to people in grief and crisis. It was especially tailored for the tragic days all of them faced in Vietnam. Finding one family who had not been touched by the war through the loss of at least one loved one would be impossible.

When I finished teaching, I felt strongly the presence of the Spirit of God. I knew that I should give an invitation for people to trust Christ or to make a decision to follow Him more closely. The people began to move forward in great numbers. Many accepted Christ for the first time; others rededicated themselves to the Lord.

After spending several hours following up on those decisions and talking with numerous people, I felt a deep sense of grief and concern among them. Many of those responding wanted to enroll immediately in the seminary extension classes. They felt a sense of urgency to tell others about Jesus. I left the next morning for the coastal city of Qui-Nhon. I was excited about what had happened but still perplexed at this unprecedented movement toward the Lord.

On arriving in Qui-Nhon I made my way to the Baptist church there in the middle of the city. Six students were enrolled in the seminary. I was to teach them how to tell other people about Jesus. When I arrived at the church, instead of six, I found 12 students in the class. I took some time to get to know these additional six students and to try to understand why they were in the class. I discovered that none of the six was a Christian. The six seminary students had invited them to attend class with them. In the process of teaching the class the six seminary students actually practiced telling the other six about Jesus. All six accepted Christ as Savior.

The next morning missionary Bob Compher took me out to a village where we had several students. When we arrived, almost the entire village was gathered in a large, open field so that I could not even locate my students. The village had no electricity and therefore no microphone or loud speakers to enable such a large crowd to hear. We found some empty soda-pop crates and stacked them up. I began teaching about Jesus. I decided not to teach the material I had prepared but simply shared the gospel with them. Literally multitudes responded to receive Christ as Savior. Again, as we counseled with many of those responding, I found a deep sense of Christ's presence working mightily in their midst.

I began to wonder what strange thing was happening to cause these multitudes of people in Danang and Qui-Nhon to show up for the seminary classes and respond so dramatically. I had taught at these various centers before; nothing like this ever had happened. While I pondered the strangeness of these situations, I went to the coastal city of Nhatrang, my last stop before returning to Saigon.

Late in the afternoon I arrived at the Baptist church ready to teach that night. The church already was filled almost to capacity.

138

When the time to begin studying arrived, the church was overflowing with people. Another missionary and I taught classes the entire evening. When we finished, no one wanted to leave. We sensed God's presence tremendously in our midst. People were in prayer and could not cease praying. All night long we continued singing and praying in the church. We experienced confession of sin, forgiveness offered and received, spontaneous tears of repentance, and thanksgiving to God. We acutely realized that all of us were standing in the very presence of Christ.

The church where we met was rather crudely equipped with wooden benches with no way to lean back. It had no restroom facilities. It was hot and overcrowded. Despite these difficulties and distractions we saw no evidence that anyone wanted to leave. The power of the Spirit of God was evident in the midst of God's people.

We had been up all night, but no one mentioned needing food and water. Early in the morning one of the leaders began to consider how we would feed everyone and sent several people to the market to buy food. I was fatigued after teaching all evening and then being up all night but strangely filled with the powerful presence of the Lord. I felt as though the Spirit of God permeated the little church and everyone there. For me, the week had been extremely tiring in these cities where so many people attended the meetings and I had spent long hours with those making decisions. They had been so hungry to know more. They had questioned rapidly and were answered rapidly, only to be followed by more questions which took us deeper into the Word of God. Even when I went to my room at night to sleep, they waited, Bible in hand, to learn more. I found a quiet place to renew my strength for the day's teaching. Now at the end of the trip we experienced the most intense meetings of all.

The classes were scheduled to meet the entire day. I wondered whether anyone would stay for the day's study after being up all night. I was amazed that after a light breakfast of French bread stuffed with pressed meat, cucumbers, and a small slice of hot pepper, everyone was back in the church and ready for the day.

Just as I stood to begin teaching, several people entered the meeting and whispered to some of the people seated in the back of the room. I could tell that excitement was in the air. I stopped and asked them to report on what was happening. They told of multitudes of people beginning to drift into the city from the central highlands. They were the first of a huge wave of refugees out the mountains. They were fleeing the onslaught of communist forces. We began to hear their stories as they told of huge numbers of communist forces sweeping through every village in the mountains. They said that masses of people were fleeing in face of this force. They told how the Vietnamese army was in full retreat, even leaving vehicles, guns, ammunition, and other equipment behind. Most of the cities in the highlands now were in communist hands. Realizing the significance of this, I boarded the first plane back to Saigon to try to get a better picture of what was happening all over the country.

In the following years I have looked back on this week on the coast of Vietnam and can see the hand of God at work in a mighty way. The people themselves clearly did not realize what was happening politically and militarily when they responded so strongly to the moving of the Spirit. We now realize that His Spirit was moving mightily to prepare His people for what was about to happen. All over Vietnam, God was bringing people to Himself and deepening the spiritual life and commitment of the Vietnam Christians, because they were about to go through the deepest crisis of their lives.

As I arrived in Saigon, the news was grim. People already were arriving in the city from all over the country. We saw that these events most likely were marking the end of freedom for the Vietnamese people. One night as I prayed, my mind went back to something that had happened just three months before this. The story began about eight years before when a young Vietnamese army captain visited Grace Baptist Church where I was pastor at that time. He told me that he had just returned to Vietnam after spending a year in training at Fort Benning in Columbus, GA. He said that while he was at the First Baptist Church there, he had trusted Jesus. He had attended church regularly while in the States and was baptized. He was not aware that in Vietnam he would find a Baptist church.

As he entered town from the airport, he passed by a church and saw the word *Baptist*. He immediately stopped the car and went in.

I was pastor of Grace Baptist Church at the time and happened to be at the church. He told me that he had graduated from Saigon University with a degree in law. He now was practicing law as a captain in the Vietnamese army. In the following years he moved up rapidly in the military ranks. He was sent to the University of Pittsburgh to get a masters degree in Business Administration. On returning to Saigon he became a prominent judge in the supreme court of Vietnam. Within two years, President Nguyen Van Thieu, president of the Republic of Vietnam, made him his special assistant. From there he became the minister of agriculture and land reform. When he became a cabinet minister, he and his wife visited our home. He said that because of security reasons he no longer could attend Grace Church. All of the security precautions would disrupt the church and place everyone in danger. He asked, "Would you be willing to visit my office every Monday morning to read the Bible with me and pray with me?" I was thrilled with this invitation and responded positively. This began years of an intimate relationship in which he grew rapidly in his Christian life.

Now, eight years later and four months before the collapse of Vietnam on an early evening in late November, I received an urgent call from this man. He asked if he and his wife could visit our home. When I heard his voice, I knew immediately that something was wrong. He seemed deeply troubled. When they entered our home, they had looks of deep concern and even fear on their faces. I noticed that his wife wept softly. He shared with me that just a few hours before, he concluded that the government of Vietnam now was totally corrupt. In light of that he could see no hope for the future of Vietnam. He said, "No country ever will be victorious if its government has such little regard for honesty and integrity." He continued, "My President whom I have faithfully served is doing nothing to correct it. Vietnam is going to collapse." He said, "This afternoon I shared this with my President and urged him to take measures to correct the situation in order to save the nation." He continued, "My President responded saying that I have two days to leave the country.

"I must leave with my entire family and never return to Vietnam. We have come to tell you good-bye and that we will be leaving for France day after tomorrow. We are deeply saddened and troubled, but the President has given me no option."

His head bowed low and his shoulders shook with the deep grief that overwhelmed him. Seeing this great man—a Supreme Court justice and a cabinet minister—so deeply grieved over his country was almost more than I could bear. I had watched him rise over the years from a young captain in the army to the highest echelons of his government. I had watched his Christian sensitivities and commitment grow and deepen. Now, the corruption and dishonesty within his government created the intense desire to see his President take steps to try to ensure a decent, honest government which could withstand the onslaught of communism. This was not to be. With that, the couple disappeared into the night. I never saw them again.

In January, the country was rapidly collapsing. My friend had been prophetic in his words to President Nguyen Van Thieu. In early April the situation had deteriorated dramatically. Despite trying to cling to the hope that Vietnam would survive, we realistically knew that the end was near. I chaired the school board for the American community school. I believed I must go to the American Embassy to talk with the ambassador and see what he would recommend. I learned that the ambassador was out of the country.

I talked with the highest official who would see me. I asked if we should go ahead and close the school, disburse the funds, and give the library to one of the local institutions. He berated me for having such little hope and assured me that America never would let Vietnam fall to the communists. He said that if we close the school, people would panic into wanting to leave Vietnam. The embassy did not want that to happen.

After I left his office, I was deeply troubled and disillusioned by his response. I was angry that he would think that I was so stupid as to believe what he was telling me. The Holy Spirit did not seem to let me take this answer. I walked out into the street and stopped at the corner under a shade tree. I just felt this tremendous urgency to pray and seek the Lord's guidance in this. As I looked up, my eyes fell immediately on the Canadian Embassy across the street. I decided to visit the Canadian ambassador and get another opinion.

142

On arrival at the Canadian embassy I was shown in to the ambassador's office. I explained the predicament of the American community school. I told him I thought that while we have time, we should dispose of the school and its properties in an orderly fashion. I asked him, "In your opinion, should we do this yet?" Without hesitation he said, "Close the school today. Begin to make preparations. This country will fall within the month. If I were you, I would begin to get all of my people out of this country." I expressed my appreciation to him and left. Within two days the school was closed, the library given to needy schools, and the money on hand disposed of according to the wishes of the school board. Again, the quiet urging of the Holy Spirit was preparing every step of the way for what was inevitable in the days ahead.

CHAPTER 15

Discussion Questions

An interesting dilemma occurs in this chapter. The Holy Spirit moved in unusual ways which could have portended a great awakening in Vietnam. However, the country was rapidly collapsing before the communist onslaught. In light of the great response, how much time and attention should Christian leaders give to evangelism and discipleship versus the need to prepare urgently necessary elements for the collapse of the country?

Use the following questions as an opportunity to discuss your own spiritual pilgrimage:

1. Why do you think the Holy Spirit was moving so dramatically among the people just before the collapse of the country?

2. What kind of impact do you think the strategy of having a maximum number of extension students over the country rather than a large resident seminary student body would have after the collapse of the country to communism?

Chapter 16

Divine Protection and Human Humor

The city of Saigon now was surrounded by communist forces. More than a million refugees had flooded into the city from all over the country. They fled before the wave of a victorious army. The American military had left Vietnam in 1973. Now, in early April, 1975, many of the remaining American government and civilian women and children began to depart. Missionaries were busy trying to help the flood of refugees who were living in makeshift shelters on sides of roads and streets, soccer fields, and wherever they could find shelter from the extremely hot sun. Most only had the clothes on their backs. Food was in short supply. The Vietnamese government was in disarray and unable to meet the needs of these masses.

The Vietnam Baptist Theological Seminary where I served as president now was filled to capacity with families taking refuge in the seminary buildings. Classes were more and more difficult to convene. The situation throughout the country evidently had deteriorated to a point beyond anyone's control. Instead of trying to continue classwork, seminary students organized to set up rice kitchens in soccer fields, on roadsides, and anywhere we could help the refugees.

Two days before Easter on Good Friday the mission office received an urgent call from missionary Bob Davis in the city of Danang. He related that the city of Danang now was seriously threatened by communist forces and the situation was deteriorating by the hour. Nearly 500 refugees had flooded into Hope Baptist Church. No food was available to feed them. He asked if bags of rice could be sent urgently by some means. Missionary Sam Longbottom and I began to try to find a way to meet this need. All roads leading to central Vietnam were blocked by communist forces. Trucks were being hijacked either by South Vietnamese troops or by the communist forces. We finally located a small shipping company which agreed to load rice onto one of its small coastal freighters and take it up the coast to Danang. The company warned that many of its small ships were being commandeered by Vietnamese military and hoards of refugees fleeing the advance of the communist forces. Loading the ship in the city of Saigon would be impossible, but if we could get the rice to the city of Long Hai near Vung Tau, they would go ashore and load it early Sunday morning. Sam Longbottom and I urgently purchased the bags of rice, loaded them onto a pickup truck, and into an old Ford van.

As we discussed the situation, we realized that no one on the ship would know where to deliver the rice. Our people in Danang would have no idea when or where the ship would arrive. I volunteered to board the ship in Long Hai and go with the rice to Danang. I then could have it unloaded and take it to the church. I realized that this was a very dangerous situation and would place my family in great anxiety, but we had no other recourse.

Early Easter Sunday morning, I packed a small bag of personal items and made my way to the mission office. Two missionaries drove the pickup truck. Sam Longbottom and I drove the van. When we reached the coast, we were notified that Vietnamese troops had commandeered the coastal freighter. It no longer was available to us. Not wanting to take the rice all the way back to Saigon and seeing the masses of refugees we took the rice to a location where a large number of refugees from the highlands were located. Permission was given by the government authorities to give the rice to these refugees. A hastily devised system of distribution was organized. By early afternoon all the rice had been distributed. We stopped at a restaurant, ate lunch, and began the trip back to Saigon. We knew that the closer to evening the more dangerous the road would be. The pickup truck left first; we followed in the van.

As we drove out of the city about 10 kilometers, we had a flat tire. We changed the tire, drove about five kilometers, and had another flat tire. I remained with the Volkswagen van, while Sam Longbottom caught a small motorized "Lambretta" (a three-wheel, motorized vehicle with seating enclosed in the back) and found a place to repair both tires. He returned with the tires repaired; we continued on our way. About 10 kilometers later we had another flat tire. The spare was put on the wheel. About 25 kilometers later we had a fifth flat tire and shortly thereafter a sixth. By now we had no more tires and were too far to return to Long Hai and not quite halfway back to Saigon. The countryside was deserted except for one house in the distance in a field. It was nearly 6 in the evening and almost dark. We would have to spend the night in the country. We walked to the nearby farm house and inquired if we could stay there for the night. The people involved were terrified. They said that the communist troops were everywhere. If the family was discovered harboring Americans, we all would be killed. They implored us to get as far away from their house as we could as quickly as we could. We knew that sleeping in the van certainly would expose us to the attention of communist soldiers who undoubtedly would search an abandoned vehicle. Sam and I began to look for a place in the nearby fields where we could hide for the night.

At dark, we saw lights of a truck approaching. We ran to the highway and attempted to flag down the truck, but it kept going at high speed. Occasional cars went by but no doubt were afraid to stop in the darkness of the night. This happened several times in the early evening. Finally, just when we despaired of catching a ride, we were able to stop an old truck. The Vietnamese driver identified himself and his family. He was a dentist from the coastal city of Vung Tau fleeing with his family to safety in Saigon. He took us to the back of the truck and told us to get in. We were amazed to see an elderly man and woman, three small children, several bags of rice, a live pig, about 10 chickens, some household furniture, two bicycles, and a dental chair completely equipped with the drill hanging over its stand and needles in the tray. The driver instructed us to get down behind the rice bags so that we could not be seen. He said that we almost certainly would be stopped by communist forces. He said discovering two Americans in the truck would spell disaster for all of us. He let us know that he was risking his life and that of his family to take us to safety.

Sam and I made a place behind the rice bags and pulled the bicycles over our heads as further concealment. We could not see anything because of the pitch blackness around us. We talked about the anxiety that our families no doubt were feeling since we had not returned with the other missionaries who had preceded us. We both regretted putting our families through such anguish. Together we prayed for safety for ourselves and for these very brave people who were risking their lives to assure our safety.

After several kilometers I felt something like rain on the top of my head. I asked Sam if he had felt any drops of rain. He said, "No, that's not possible. This is a covered truck. You must be mistaken." I remarked that we were not in the rainy season, so this cannot be rain. A few moments later he said, "You're right. Something is falling, but it's not rain. The consistency doesn't feel like water." I felt the top of my head and realized that what was there wasn't rain. The chickens had begun to roost on the bicycle wheels above our head and began dropping their excrement on us. We both began to laugh hysterically as though hours of pent-up anxiety was finding a moment of release. We spent the rest of the trip trying to shoo the chickens away from the bicycles, only to have them return immediately to their favorite roosting place!

At around nine o'clock the truck dropped us off in front of the mission office. Lights were on in the office. We made our way inside. All the missionaries in town were there having special prayer for our safe return. The missionaries who preceded us home had alerted all the families of their concern that something may have happened to us. Seeing these two men enter the room with hair unkempt, clothes disheveled, dirty faces and hands, and smelling of a barnyard must have been a sight. Despite that we had a glorious reunion, though some hesitated to hug us even in their exuberance.

For all of us, these various experiences of danger and anxiety had become all too frequent. However, the result was that it drew all of us closer together as a mission family. Our lives became filled with intense prayer and a constant, total dependence and trust in the perfect will of the Lord. We truly became one body, closely knit together in Christ. These times would shape our faith, our worldview, and our lives forever.

CHAPTER 16

Discussion Questions

This chapter presents not so much a dilemma but several responses required to meet an almost hopeless situation—Danang surrounded by hostile forces and 500 people in the church complex without food. How do you feed them? No transportation, in a rural area with night approaching, infested with enemy troops, and wanting to go home. How do you find a secure place? How do you get home?

In view of the chapter you just read, use the following questions as an opportunity to discuss your own spiritual pilgrimage as a follower of Jesus:

1. How do you respond to seemingly hopeless situations? Do you tend to panic and seek a response, or do you turn it into the hands of God and offer yourself as an instrument in His hands to resolve the problem?

2. Sometimes even in the direst circumstances will be opportunities to see humor which will defuse the tension. In this story it was "roosting chickens." Sometimes God provides an opportunity for humor to give us relief and release if we but look for it. Have you noticed humor in some of the situations you have faced?

3. Having the kind of friends who gather to pray at the least sign of threat or danger, even as this story reveals, is important. Making relationships while we are safe and secure prepares us to have friends when things do not go well and the need for prayer is great. On whom would you call? Who is such a friend that no prompting is needed to bring about concentrated intense prayer when it is needed?

Chapter 17

Identity Lost and Found

The time to leave had arrived. I don't know exactly how I knew, but the feeling was unmistakable. Rachel and the children had left Vietnam about three weeks previously. My heart was torn. On the one hand, I wanted to stay even after the communists assumed control. I wanted to be with our people in a very dark and uncertain hour. On the other hand, my family would be intensely anxious, since no telephone connections were possible and they temporarily lived in far-away Taiwan. I couldn't let them know whether or not I was safe. I had no way to know whether my continued presence in Vietnam would bring harm to other Christians there after the communists took control. The decision to leave was the most heart-rending one that I ever had to make. Opposing forces now surrounded the city of Saigon.

The day was in the middle of April, 1975. The weather was stifling hot. On such hot days everything always seemed quieter and slower than usual. However, the quiet during this day was as though everything was waiting silently in dreadful anticipation of something terrible about to happen. I realized painfully that nearly 14 years of my life had been spent serving the Lord among a people I had grown to respect and love dearly. Now through no choice of my own that relationship was violently ending.

Every morning when I arose I would see crowds of people gathered outside of my front gate. During the years I had hated the fact that I lived behind a wall with a high gate that seemed to seal me off from my Vietnamese neighbors all around. This was done for protection in a country at war where so many unexpected things can happen in such a brief moment. During these turbulent days that wall became a welcome source of protection. I could hardly bear to look out of my upstairs window on the scene below and see the

149

masses of people gathered at my gate. Everyone in the community knew that I was a pastor—an American missionary. They knew that I held that precious U.S. passport; that meant that I surely would be leaving Vietnam. Many believed that if they could just get their babies or their little children into my hands, I would take them out of the country to safety.

I faced this scene morning after morning as I tried to leave my home for whatever task was ahead of me during each day of this crisis. I felt tremendously hurt when a Christian brother or sister would visit and bring their beautiful children. With tears streaming down their faces these parents would implore me to take with me their children out of the country. I hurt when I had to say I had no other choice but to refuse. One morning a middle-aged woman saw me leaving my home. Before I could open the gate, she climbed the wall and literally threw her 2-year-old child over it. I had to run as quickly as I could to try to catch this child before she hit the ground. I carried the child as rapidly as I could through the streets to catch the mother before she was lost from sight. When I finally caught up with her, she refused to take the child back. I had to leave this little one crying in the street. That was painful!

The seminary and the mass-communications studio were situated on the same property. Missionary Peyton Moore was in charge of mass communications. He and I decided that we would call all employees together. We believed that Vietnamese employees would be in danger if communists knew they were working for Americans. We gave them a choice of taking several months of their pay in money or rice and leaving immediately in order to distance themselves from us, or staying and taking the chance that some miracle might occur and we could remain in Vietnam and continue the work. We gathered everyone into a room and asked these faithful Christian employees to express themselves on a secret ballot. When the ballots were counted, 100 percent of the employees vowed to stay on and serve the Lord with us in spite of the risk to their lives.

One afternoon, when I was in my temporary office in the rear of the seminary, my secretary ran into my office with blood on her face and streaming down on her Vietnamese dress. Her face was badly bruised. She was trembling all over and crying. She implored me to get out of the building. I had turned the seminary over to our young dean, Mr. Dao Van Chinh, a graduate of the seminary, and moved my office from the administration building to a small area on the back of the property. He now occupied the president's office. My secretary told how five young men, certainly soldiers, had appeared at her desk and asked for the American president of the seminary. She told them that I was not present and no longer was president of the seminary. They insisted that my car was in the driveway and therefore I must be there. She showed them the president's office. She explained that the new Vietnamese president was in the city doing business for the seminary. They kicked the office door open and confirmed that no one was there. They then hit her, knocked her to the floor, and vowed to return. I knew then that my continued presence was endangering the lives of all who worked there. The time for me to leave had arrived.

Each night was a time of decision. At night the sounds of gunfire could be heard all around the city. Sometimes firing was particularly intense. I would wonder if the final attack was beginning. I was alone in our home. Nights were particularly frightening as I lay alone and wondered what would happen. I pondered over and over again whether I should try to stay even after the new government took over. Would this endanger those who were associated with us? Would I be allowed to do anything at all? Would they imprison American missionaries as had happened in other situations similar to this? All of these questions were relevant. I knew that my wife and children were safe in Taiwan, but they had no way of knowing whether I was safe. Months of anxiety and worry about my safety could occur. Was I right to put them through this kind of anxiety? I lay there pondering these things until dawn arrived. The sound of birds singing and children playing in the street brought a renewed sense of tranquility. Each morning I decided to stay one more day.

The refugee population in the city swelled to more than a million pouring in from all across the country. These people had no food, no water, and no place to stay. They were like sheep without a shepherd and no hope for tomorrow. They were searching for some way out. The city of Saigon had become their last hope. Fear and panic were on their faces. We knew that feeding stations needed to be set up all around the city. We were grateful when, at our request, the Southern Baptist Foreign Mission Board, as it was known then, sent $25,000 to help feed the multitudes. Every seminary student was involved in this undertaking. The seminary building and grounds were filled with refugees. Classes were suspended. All efforts were given to caring for the homeless. Leaving the country with all these needs was not easy.

The young pastor of Grace Baptist Church in Saigon, Rev. Le Quoc Chanh, with his wife and little child visited me on a Friday night. They said they had an opportunity to get a boat out of the country. They were going to spend the weekend praying about leaving. I pledged to join them in prayer. He was such a wonderful young man and a great servant of the Lord in the churches. On the one hand I wanted him to stay and continue to minister to the needy people and keep the name of Jesus everpresent in Vietnam. Faithful Christian servants like Rev. Chanh and his wife would preserve the church in Vietnam during the dark days ahead. On the other hand I knew that his days as a minister may be short. He might never be permitted to serve the Lord again. No one could predict what the communist government would do with religions. Past history indicated a future of persecution and suffering. I wanted to pray for him to leave while he could. My inner tension as I prayed was intense.

On the following Monday this young pastor and his wife returned to my home. They immediately began sharing the conviction of their heart. "All weekend we prayed earnestly for God's will to be made known," he told me. "We have concluded that God called us to be a shepherd and has given us a flock of sheep and put them in our care. Just as the Good Shepherd could not run away from His responsibility, neither can we." He knew that the future of the Christians in his church was fraught with danger; he could not leave them. With that firm conviction they decided to stay and commit themselves in Jesus' name to whatever the future would hold for them. With one last statement he said, "I know that God loves us with an eternal love. Nothing can separate us from that love. His will is perfect. We cast ourselves completely into his hands for His perfect will to be done in our lives even as in the lives of our Christians." So, the decision to leave or stay was not just a decision for foreigners to make but was faced by millions of people. It was an especially agonizing decision for those who were in the Lord's service.

The hour arrived when I knew I would have to leave. I walked through each room of the house. I could hear the happy voices of my children. I went into their bedroom and looked at their clothes unique to each one. I picked up a favorite toy of each one and held it fondly. I looked at their beds and remembered how many times I had sat beside them as they prepared for sleep and told stories or listened to their concerns of the day. I felt the full impact of the memories of their young lives spent almost entirely in that country which had been our home all of those years.

I looked in our bedroom and remembered the wonderful moments Rachel and I had shared. Her clothes were hanging in the closet as she had left them. I went over and touched each dress and felt the closeness to her. I looked at our things neatly folded in the dresser drawers. I walked through a small area where my books stood in rows on a huge bookshelf the size of the wall. Books from college and three graduate-degree programs, along with other books collected through many years, lined the shelves.

I then walked to the front door, took one last, longing look, closed it, and locked it. I locked it because I had the persistent hope that just maybe I would need to leave only for a few weeks and then, by some miracle, the opportunity to return would come. Deep down I knew that I was leaving for good the collection of years of family possessions.

As I stood there in those final moments, I realized that I might lose all material possessions, but I never could lose the precious memories of years of life together. Each day we build a precious reservoir of history which can become like a fresh spring of water to drink from during times when life is dry and losing its meaning or when times are dark and confusing. We draw strength from the times when we were victorious or experienced joy or when we have been stretched beyond our ability to endure but somehow made it through. Now I was looking back into that history, drawing from its memories, and searching for answers and meaning.

Just before locking the door I knelt there in the doorway and thanked God for calling us to this place and giving us such wonderful experiences in His service which would strengthen our lives for the rest of our days.

Missionaries Bob Davis, Peyton Moore, and I met at the airport, which was mass bedlam with so many people wanting to leave. Debris lay scattered on the floor of the terminal. A gaping hole in the roof where a rocket had hit was being temporarily repaired. Through the crowds I saw a friend that I had led to the Lord and baptized. He worked for Air Vietnam. I approached him. He asked, "Pastor, are you leaving?" I replied, "Yes, I have finally decided that the time is here." "Where are you going?" he asked. One Cathay Pacific plane was parked near the terminal. "Where is that plane going?" I asked. He replied, "To Manila." I then said, "We are going to Manila!" He promised to get us seats on that plane. Some time later he approached us with three tickets which he had somehow arranged. My fellow missionary had a briefcase filled with Vietnamese money. He took out the money to pay for the tickets. My Vietnamese friend said, "No. I am sorry. We cannot accept Vietnamese money." We asked about writing a check. The reply was no. Between the three of us we did not have enough American cash to pay for the tickets. I then asked, "Will you take an American Express card?" He said, "Certainly. Give it to me." With that we held tickets which might or might not be worth anything. All was in confusion. I never received the bill from American Express.

The departure was delayed time and again. Authorities were concerned that if the masses of people saw us boarding the plane, they would rush the plane en masse and prevent the plane from taking off. Periodic firing was occurring; the plane would be an easy target during daylight hours. Darkness fell; the hour was late. I constantly was tempted to return to my home. I believed that I was abandoning my precious friends and the Vietnamese people to whom God had divinely called me to minister. I then remembered

154

the danger that my presence was bringing to them. I again thought of the agony that my wife and children would go through as I was separated from them and had no way to make contact. Each time I prayed, I was convinced that I should leave.

Finally, around 9 word arrived that we were to board the plane. The terminal, the surrounding area, and the runway were completely dark. A few rockets had landed around the airport. Any point of light would be a target for the communist forces surrounding the airport. Because of the darkness, we had to place a hand on the shoulder of the person in front and follow in a single line to reach the plane.

With rockets and mortars shooting periodically we had no way of knowing the runway condition. We were frightened to realize that the plane was taking off in total darkness with no lights on the plane or runway and no way to know whether we could take off safely.

As the plane banked over Saigon, I looked down on the city that had been my home for the better part of nearly 14 years. Here we had reared our four children. Here we had started a theological seminary and had graduated numerous wonderful, new pastors. Here I had taken the seminary students out to various places to start new churches. Here I had received word that my father had died; here I processed that grief. Here I performed weddings for young people and then visited their homes when children were born. Here young couples visited me when trouble entered their marriage and they needed counsel. Here teen-agers and college students visited my home to have new vistas of life opened to them. Here boyfriends and girlfriends visited for some loving care and advice when their hearts were broken. Here I buried loved ones of Christians and non-Christians, especially young Vietnamese soldiers killed in battle. I shared in the sorrows with their families at funerals. Here American servicemen visited our home to find relief from the tension of war. Here I wrote many letters to widows of American servicemen sharing that their loved one had been in our home or at church shortly before dying violently. Here I had seen countless people trust Jesus Christ and experience the joy and peace of knowing Him. This in every sense of the word was home.

As I looked down on the dark landscape below, here and there I could see smoke ascending from fires caused by occasional rockets that had been sent indiscriminately into the city. Suddenly I was filled with an oppressive nostalgia and feelings of sadness and grief that sent tears pouring down my cheeks. I had a tremendous urge to try to stop the plane and go back to the place that I loved so dearly and where I had found my identity for such a long time. I was filled with doubts. Was I leaving too early? Should I have stayed longer? These doubts were to plague me for years to come.

The plane circled the city and now was winging its way in the darkness toward the South China Sea. I took out my little New Testament with the psalms in the back. Turning on the overhead light, I began reading passages indiscriminately. I finally turned to Psalm 137. In the days before I departed from Vietnam, this psalm seemed to have a special message for me. "By the rivers of Babylon, there we sat down and wept, when we remembered Zion. Upon the willows in the midst of it We hung our harps. For there our captors demanded of us songs, And our tormentors mirth, saying, Sing us one of the songs of Zion." "How can we sing the Lord's song in a foreign land?" In this psalm the children of Israel were carried away captive. They were being forced to leave their beloved homeland. Their identity was inseparably tied to this land that God had promised them. Their ancestors had fought over it. Through great miracles and at a high price they had claimed it. They had built their temple in that land which further strengthened their identity as a people of God. Now, without their promised land and their temple they suffered a severe identity crisis. No wonder they wept and were unable to sing! I thought of my own identity at this point in my historical pilgrimage. For years people had asked, "Sam, who are you?" I replied with a great pride and joy, "I am a missionary in the Republic of South Vietnam."

Again, they asked, "Sam, who are you?" I replied, "I am the president of the Vietnam Theological Seminary with 130 students studying all over the country." Again, "Sam, who are you?" My reply, "I am the pastor of Faith Church—one of the churches that my students and I brought into being and which I love dearly."

Again, "Sam, who are you?" "I am the one who lives on the corner of a small street in a totally Vietnamese community and who every one in the community calls 'pastor.'" Every time people, mostly Buddhists, pass by my house, they greet me with, "Hello, pastor." I am not really their pastor in a formal sense, but I am their pastor in a personal and community sense. These identities are important to me. They signify my meaning in life. They tell volumes about my history, my present, and my future.

Now, in a matter of moments, every one of these identities had been stripped from me. None any longer could identify who I was. I no longer was a missionary in the Republic of South Vietnam. The seminary no longer existed for me. The churches were on their own. My little house on the corner was dark and empty. I felt as though I were standing naked before God with nothing to identify me.

"Sam, who are you?" someone will ask. "I do not really know," I would have to reply. Every identity I have counted dear has been stripped from me. "You see, I am crossing my river Babylon. I feel like a captive in a foreign land. I have no real identity any longer. Will I ever again be able to sing the song of the Lord?"

I know that some people cross their own Babylon every day. The death of a husband or wife plunges the remaining spouse into a new identity crisis. The forced move by a corporation from one city to another brings identity crisis to the whole family. The loss of a job can devastate in its impact on identity. Many lose their fortunes every year because of sudden and unexpected changes in economic conditions. With each recession many lose their businesses and life savings. Divorce is a devastating identity crisis especially where children are involved. A weak moment of moral lapse may create an identity crisis lasting for a lifetime. Rivers of Babylon await all of us at some point in life. The experience can devastate.

As I sat contemplating, slowly the Holy Spirit began to clarify. "Sam, who are you?" the voice asks. "I am a child of God," I reply. "Through the death and resurrection of Jesus Christ and through His power to save, I have transcended geography and history and the here and now. I have an eternal identity which life circumstances never can change or remove. It never can be taken from me. The only way I can lose this identity is if I, myself, lay it down. The only One who could remove it from me is God Himself, because it is my gift from Him for eternity."

I switched off the light above my head, closed my Bible, and sat in the darkness listening to the drone of the engines as we winged across the South China Sea. In the darkness of those moments I pledged that never again would titles that people or organizations give constitute my identity. Never again would a vocational calling reveal who I am. Never again would a geographical location be of such importance. By the grace of God my walk with Jesus, my behavior, my attitude, my commitment of life, my very being will reveal one singular identity. I am God's child for eternity.

CHAPTER 17

Discussion Questions

This chapter is filled with significant dilemmas which produced inner conflict and intense emotions. To leave or not to leave was a dilemma. To encourage and help people to leave Vietnam or to provide no encouragement or help was another dilemma. To keep employees on the job and thus risk their lives or to provide them with assistance and allow them to leave for their own security was a dilemma. To surrender identity or to try to hold on to identity at any price was a significant conflict.

In view of the chapter you just read, use the following questions as an opportunity to discuss your own spiritual pilgrimage as a follower of Jesus:

1. What determines your sense of identity? How do you want those around you to know you?

2. After reading the chapter, do you think the author would have been right to have remained in Vietnam to see what would happen? Was he right to leave?

3. How does your personal history affect your life? Is it a strengthening influence? Is it a history from which, because of its trauma, you need to learn? Is it a history that provides a stable foundation on which to build a future life? What are you doing with your history?

Chapter 18

From Physical Rags to Spiritual Riches

With all this history in our pounding hearts, we now braced our-selves for the rough-looking men who approached us at the zoo that day in Saigon after missionary Bob Davis and I returned to Vietnam for the first time in 14 years. We did not know what this group had in mind as it moved toward us in this somewhat hidden area, but fearing the worst was easy to do.

To our great surprise and relief, these men literally fell on Bob and me, weeping and laughing and greeting us warmly. As I looked into their eyes, I began to recognize them. They were my seminary students at the time of the fall of Vietnam. The 14 years just past had not treated them kindly. They had spent years in agricultural camps at forced labor, some imprisoned, all of them frail from hunger and hard work. Their faces were weather-beaten, deeply wrinkled, their hands rough, but all with beautiful smiles. When I had known them they were young, eager to learn, fresh in their faith, and filled with hope.

My mind raced back to the first day I met them as they arrived at the seminary to study. They were from the coast of Vietnam from very poor families and with little formal education. The missionary who ministered in that area had called and asked me if he could send some students to study at the seminary. He told me that they had little education, were from a rough background, and were new Christians. He described them as very "raw, undiscipled stuff." He said that I would have my hands full trying to disciple them, but he really needed to have trained workers. Our seminary guidelines required students to be Christians at least a year and to have a mini-mum of a grade-school education to get into the certificate course. We expected them to have been involved in planting a church or serving as pastors of churches before arriving at the seminary. At

160

the very least they needed experience serving in some capacity which would enable us to assess their potential for future service.

I had explained to him that these students did not meet a single requirement for entrance. I did not find any way I could accept them, given the policies of the seminary. He continued to plead his case that he needed them trained quickly and returned to the coast to serve the Lord. The Holy Spirit seemed to compel me to accept them. I told him that I would make a special class for them and would do the best we could. I asked, "When can I expect them to arrive?" To my amazement he responded, "I put them on the bus very early this morning. They should arrive within the hour."

That began a year of great turmoil, trial, and tribulation. They tested every rule the seminary had established. They struggled to read the materials. They had experienced little church involvement or Christian teaching. They, even on occasion, stole from one another. On one occasion missing library books were found at the street market for sale. I was convinced that one or more of them had sold the books there. They simply did not understand what the Christian life was all about.

However, the one thing they seemed to have was a new and dynamic faith in Jesus. They knew that they had been sent to the seminary to be trained to serve Him. What that meant in terms of Christian living they did not know, but being at the seminary was better than anything else offered to them. I spent hours helping them to understand that Christians just do not do some things. Some other things Christians must do. These students knew little about Christian tradition and Christian concepts of morality. They indeed were "raw material."

They knew little about living in the city and about how city people behave. I took them out into the streets and narrow alleyways of the city to witness. I read the Scripture with them and prayed with them. I tried to find every way to nurture them. At times I was encouraged and felt surges of hope. At times I despaired that they would ever make any kind of servants for the Lord. They arrived at the seminary in September, 1974. The attacks which led to the collapse of the Vietnamese government began in late January,

1975. By early April, the situation in Saigon was such that we had to call off classes and begin to spend all of our time helping the more than one million refugees pouring into the city fleeing the advancing communist forces.

These young men joined in the work hauling bags of rice and setting up places in which people could cook. Together we located soccer fields, empty lots, and anywhere we could provide steamed rice and other nourishment for hoards of people living in whatever empty space they could find. When difficult work and long hours were involved, these young men were ready and prepared to do whatever was necessary.

These young men only had about six months of seminary training before classes were dismissed. Even on the night I left Vietnam, my heart was heavy as I thought of these new students. My mind was flooded with regrets that these young men never would get the training for which they so longed. I wondered what would happen to them. Would they continue to be faithful? Would they find ways to serve the Lord?

Through all of those years of absence I thought about them and wondered about them. Now, suddenly, here they were, standing in this little clearing in the midst of a jungle, crying and laughing, hugging and gesturing, all talking at the same time and eager to tell what had happened over those years.

Bob Davis and I sat there with them around the table and listened intently as they told their stories of faithfulness, of sacrificial service to the Lord, of all that God had done during those 14 long years. We discovered that all of them were leading numerous house churches which they themselves had started. They were teaching and discipling large numbers of people. God was using them in miraculous ways.

We continued talking for several hours. I sat in rapt amazement at what they were telling me. They had walked through deep struggles of prison and agricultural communes, persecution, trials, hardships, hunger, and loneliness. Yet God always had kept them mindful of His presence. By their testimony, at times all they had left was Jesus, but He was sufficient for all of their needs.

At a point in the conversation, everyone became silent. One of the men picked up a paper bag and opened it. He pulled out an old aluminum tray and placed it in the center of the table. Another one opened a paper bag, pulled out a loaf of bread, and placed it on the tray. Another opened a bag and pulled out a handful of grapes. He placed them on the tray.

One of the men stood up. Without saying a word he broke the loaf of bread in two and passed it around the table. We each took a small piece. Another passed the grapes; we each took one. Another one stood and prayed one of the most beautiful prayers I ever have experienced. We each ate the bread. Another stood and prayed; we ate the grapes. No one even mentioned that this was a service of communion, or the Lord's Supper, or a religious ritual. Yet, no one could doubt that what we were doing was uniting ourselves together after a long separation, remembering as we broke the bread the broken body of our Lord and as we ate the grapes, His blood poured out on the cross for each of us.

It was a time of silent confession, of forgiveness, of cementing relationships, of acknowledging the very presence of our Lord. Without anyone speaking we stood together and joined hands. Then each of the men slowly disappeared back into the underbrush.

Bob and I walked out of the zoo in reflective silence. Now I knew what had happened to these men who at one time I had almost turned aside but who the Spirit of God would not let me deny. God had taken each of them and in His own way trained them and molded them into His image. God had taken these men whose lives and backgrounds seemed to offer such little promise and had made them to become beautiful instruments in His hand to bring countless people to know Jesus.

I realized that these men were not much different from the first disciples Jesus called. They would have met none of the criteria to be leaders. Yet through the miraculous power of God those disciples brought the world face to face with Jesus. Our criteria and standards are not always God's criteria and standards. People look on the outward appearance, but God looks on the heart. People judge and conclude based on what they see and know by their own standards.

God always is giving a chance—an opportunity for us to allow Him to make us into what He would have us to be. Ultimately, whatever transformation occurs is because of God's great power in us to change us, to energize us, to strengthen us, and to give us His authority to overcome and having overcome to be victorious.

The astounding thing was that I, the teacher, the model, the discipler, had been led into the very presence of the Lord by my students, who now were modeling for me the very presence of Christ. In a true sense of the word, they were discipling me. I know of no greater blessing than to experience first-hand in the living flesh the miraculous power of God transforming lives into the very image of Christ.

What I had entrusted to God as I left Vietnam in those heart-rending, agonizing days in 1975, He had graciously multiplied and used a thousand-fold. He had allowed me to be a servant on the edge of history. What joy I had in seeing fruit borne in the lives of these and others like them!

CHAPTER 18

Discussion Questions

This last chapter presents the condition of the fellowship of Christians some 14 years after the collapse of Vietnam and my involvement there. That the church of our Lord was still alive attests to the faithfulness of the Holy Spirit to work in the lives of believers even under the most harsh of conditions. To think that just because "missionaries" no longer are present means the church will weaken or die is the height of human pride. History reveals to us that the church always grows in strength and multiplies itself under harsh conditions of persecution. Vietnam has been no exception.

This last chapter has some interesting truths. First, God can take any person, anywhere, any time, under any conditions, and mold him or her into the kind of servant He wants that person to be. Second, the bonds between Christian believers are so strong that they transcend time and geography. When the opportunity presents itself, an easy renewal of fellowship and strengthening of the bond occurs. Third, foreign finances, outside human assistance, lack of formal education, and beautiful buildings never have determined the health of the church. That is determined by the faithfulness of believers and the work of the Holy Spirit within them.

Use the following questions as an opportunity to discuss your own spiritual pilgrimage as a follower of Jesus.

1. Have you encountered people who have become followers of Jesus but whose lives show little promise of effective service to the Lord? How do you relate to them in the formation of their spiritual life? What is the best way to relate to them?

2. Many denominations and individual Christians believe that the Lord's Supper, or communion, is reserved for the local, organized church. Some people believe that only an ordained pastor is to preside. The experience this chapter describes differs greatly from that. It never was termed "the Lord's Supper", but in essence, it was. Should I have advised the participants that they were in some sort of error, taken that opportunity to teach them, and refused to participate? What would you have done, and why?

ABOUT THE AUTHOR

Born: May 25, 1932, in Liberty, NC

Education: Received the bachelor of arts degree (*cum laude*), with majors in Classical Greek and History, from Wake Forest University, Winston Salem, NC, and the master of divinity, master of theology in New Testament interpretation, and doctor of ministry in pastoral counseling degrees from Southeastern Baptist Theological Seminary, Wake Forest, NC. Chaplain intern and resident, North Carolina Memorial Hospital, Chapel Hill, 1971-73. Center for Creative Leadership (Executive Management Course/Workshop), Eckard College, 1985, and Foundations of Leadership Workshop, 1997, and certified by the Center for Creative Leadership, Greensboro, NC, as executive feedback specialist, 1996. Feedback specialist for the Center for Creative Leadership Development and the International Centre for Excellence in Leadership, 1997.

Married: Rachel Kerr of Durham, NC

Children: Deborah, Stephen, Philip, and Michael are grown.

Prior Experience: Pastor of Mount Pleasant Baptist Church, Liberty, NC

Founded: Homestead Heights Baptist Church, (now named "The Summit") Durham, NC. Served six years in the United States Navy, with service in the Korean War.

Published: Authored "Training for Urban Evangelization" in *An Urban World*, edited by Larry Rose and Kirk Hadaway. Authored a chapter entitled "The Church in the War-torn Vietnam Society," 25th Anniversary Bulletin, Asia Baptist Graduate Theological Seminary.

Overseas Experience: Appointed missionary in March, 1962, by the International Mission Board, SBC, for general evangelism in the Republic of South Vietnam. Served as English-language evangelist in Kowloon, Hong Kong, 1962, while awaiting visas for Vietnam; language study, Dalat, Vietnam, 1962-64; director of theological education and pastor of one church and planter of five others, 1964-1975; founder and president of Vietnam Baptist

Theological Seminary, Saigon, 1964-1975; faculty member and trustee for Asia Baptist Graduate Theological Seminary, 1965-80, and chairman of the committee to design the first doctor of ministry degree tailored for Asian pastors and scholars, 1974.

After leaving Vietnam following the communist assumption of control of Vietnam, he went to Guam to aid in refugee efforts with Southeast Asian refugees. Served as field representative for East Asia, stationed in Taiwan, 1976-80; in 1980, he became director of the Missionary Learning Department, where he was responsible for the programs of orientation and equipping of missionaries throughout the world; Designed the philosophy, programs, and led the design of the Missionary Learning Center, Rockville, VA, a $50,000,000 training center for the 5,500 overseas missionaries of the International Mission Board.

In 1985, he became area director for East Asia, living in Hong Kong, and directing work in Korea, Japan, Taiwan, Hong Kong, and Macau. In 1992 he became regional vice president for Europe, the Middle East, and Northern Africa after the collapse of communism in Eastern Europe. In 1994 he became vice president for Creative Leadership Development, assuming responsibility for all of the Board's orientation, training and equipping programs for adults and children, and founding The International Centre for Excellence in Leadership. Since 1995 he has served as liaison to Baptist seminaries across the United States.

From 1994-2001 he served on the Overseas Leadership Team that oversees the work of 5,200 Southern Baptist missionaries among more than 220 people groups around the world.

On February 25, 2002, he retired from the staff of the International Mission Board and accepted immediate ISC appointment to Southeast Asia to serve in Vietnam. During the Iraq war he was transferred to the Middle East and Northern Africa to serve in the area of member care, where he continues to serve.

He has served as spiritual retreat and Bible-conference speaker, and conducted leadership-development workshops for missionaries and nationals in more than 90 countries around the world.

PHOTO ALBUM

Original home of Grace Baptist Church (Vietnamese) and Trinity Baptist Church (English). Grace Church was the first Baptist church organized in Vietnam. November, 1962.

Service of organization of Grace Baptist Church in Saigon, November, 1962. Missionaries Lewis Myers and Bill Roberson are in the foreground.

The first worship service in Dalat, Vietnam—Easter, 1964.

Sam Longbottom, left; Sam James, 1965.

Vietnam Baptist Mission, 1965. Front row, from left: Peyton Moore, Celia Moore, Margaret Gayle, Toni Myers, Walter Routh. Second row: Bob Compher, Sam James, Priscilla Compher, Pauline Routh, Rachel James, Audrey Roberson, Dottie Hayes. Third row: Lewis Myers, Jim Gayle, Betty Merrell, Ron Merrell, Bill Roberson, Fred Linkenhoyer (journeyman), Herman Hayes.

Pastor Le Quoc Chanh, new mission church, 1965. Later pastor, Grace Church (Chapter 17).

168

Rachel's Grace Church children's choir, Saigon, 1965 (Chapter 11). Miss Phuc is directing.

Earliest residential seminary class, Thu Duc, Vietnam, 1967: Thai Luong Quoc, Do Huy Hy, Do Vinh Thanh (Chapter 5, 6), Le Quoc Trung, Le Quoc Chanh, Le Van Hoa, Sam James (seminary president).

House church (later Petrusky Baptist Church) in Mr. and Mrs. Chieu's home. At upper left is Rachel James and Mrs. Chieu's 90-year-old mother, who later was baptized at age 91. Mrs. Chieu is in the right upper corner. Mrs. Chieu's daughter, Be, is in the center of the photo. See the story of this house church in Chapter 13.

At left, Mrs. Chieu's mother.

At right, house church in Mr. and Mrs. Chieu's home. Sam and Rachel James in foreground. Sam holds Be.

169

First graduation ceremony of the Vietnam Baptist Theological Seminary, May, 1970, Saigon. Sam James, seminary president, presiding. Missionary Earl Bengs is to Sam's right, and Missionary Carl Hunker, president of the Taiwan Theological Seminary, is to Sam's left. Next to Hunker is Do Huy Hy and Do Vinh Thanh. Pastor Thanh's story is in Chapters 5-6.

Pastor and Mrs.Thanh with their son, Tu. Tu's story is found in Chapters 5-6.

First graduation ceremony of the Vietnam Baptist Theological Seminary, 1970, Saigon. Sam James presents diploma to Mr. Do Huy Hy. Pastor Do Vinh Thanh stands next to Mr. Hy. Pastor Thanh's father, also a pastor, is in the foreground.

At left, Rev. Thanh preaching in makeshift shelter to begin what became the Faith Baptist Church in Saigon.

At right, typical Vietnamese elderly man dressed similarly to Rev. Thanh's father and father-in-law. Their story is in Chapter 6.

Rev. Thanh leads children's choir for a children's service at Faith Baptist Church, Gia Dinh.

Rachel James at mission point clinic, 1968.

170

At left: Rachel James at the "Baptist Halfway House", a daytime home for extremely poor and orphaned children, Gia Dinh, Vietnam, 1974.

Below: Missionary-national Christian gathering at Grace church, Saigon, 1973. Front row, from left: Priscilla Tunnell, Betty Merrell, Pam Williams, Celia Moore, Rachel James (face hidden). Back row, from left: Peyton Moore, Walter Routh, R. Keith Parks (area secretary for Southeast Asia).

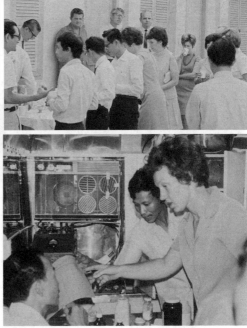

Above: Sam James and Mr. An several months after Mr. An became a follower of Christ. Mr. An's story is in Chapters 7, 8, and 9.

At right: Rachel James in her mobile clinic in Gia Dinh, March, 1975. Below: Street scene in Saigon showing many transportation modes.

At right: The James family, 1972. From left: Michael, Rachel, Sam, Philip, Stephen, and Deborah.

171

Sam James preparing to deliver rice to refugees in Long Hai, Vietnam, April, 1975 (Easter Sunday before Vietnam collapsed on April 30). See Chapter 16.

First of five flat tires on Easter Sunday, April, 1975, on road from Long Hai to Saigon (story is in Chapter 16).

Above: Sam James, left, and Sam Longbottom negotiating rice delivery to refugees, April, 1975.

Below: Refugees fleeing communist offensive in last days of Vietnam, April, 1975 (Chapter 17).

Above: Modern Saigon—statue of Ho Chi Minh, with Municipal Building in background.

Modern Saigon—Dalat Market, March, 2000.

Modern Saigon—Saigon Catholic Cathedral.

Modern Saigon—Saigon Center for Fine Arts.

Grace Baptist Church, Saigon, November, 2003.

From left to right: Thai Luong Quoc, Pham Hong Long, Le Van Tot, unidentified, Nguyen Son, unidentified, Bui Duc Anh Tuan.

173

Grace Baptist Church adult choir, November, 2003.

Grace Baptist Church children's choir, November, 2003.

Outstanding Baptist leaders: From left to right: Pastor Le Quoc Chanh, pastor, Grace Baptist Church, Saigon; Pastor Nguyen Lanh, and director of education for a network of Baptist churches; Mrs. Do Vinh Thanh, stepmother of Tu and director of Baptist Women for Vietnam; unidentified church leader; and Mrs. Le Quoc Chanh. Taken in November, 2003.

Sam and Rachel James at the Missionary Learning Center, Rockville, VA, March, 2002.

Order more copies of

Servant on the Edge of History

Call toll free: **1-800-747-0738**

Visit: www.hannibalbooks.com
Email: hannibalbooks@earthlink.net
FAX: 1-888-252-3022
Mail copy of form below to:
Hannibal Books
P.O. Box 461592
Garland, Texas 75046

Number of copies desired _____
Multiply number of copies by $12.95 _____

Please add $3 for postage and handling for first book and add
50-cents for each additional book in the order.
Shipping and handling$_____
Texas residents add 8.25% ($1.07) sales tax $_____

Total order $_____

Mark method of payment:
check enclosed _____
Credit card# _____
exp. date____ (Visa, MasterCard, Discover, American Express accepted)

Name _____

Address _____

City State, Zip _____

Phone _____ FAX _____

Email _____

You'll enjoy these missions books also

Be a 24/7 Christian by Wade Akins. Want to make Jesus truly the Lord your life but don't know how? This renowned missionary evangelist/strategist tells how to live the adventure of being totally sold out to the Lord every moment of every day, every day of every year.

_____Copies at $9.95=_____

Rescue by Jean Phillips. American missionaries Jean Phillips and husband Gene lived through some of the most harrowing moments in African history of the last half century. Abducted and threatened with death, Jean and Gene draw on God's lessons of a lifetime.

_____Copies at $12.95=_____

Unmoveable Witness by Marion Corley. An alarming interrogation by Colombia's version of the FBI. A dangerous mishap at a construction site. A frightening theft at his home in Bucaramanga, Colombia. What kept Marion and Evelyn Corley on the mission field for 22 years when others might have returned to Stateside comforts?

_____Copies at $9.95=_____

Beyond Surrender by Barbara J. Singerman. A dramatic story of one family's quest to bring light to a dark and desperate world. The Singerman family serves in Benin, West Africa. They confront spiritual warfare beyond anything they expect when they surrender to missions.

_____Copies at $12.95=_____

Add $3.00 shipping for first book, plus 50-cents for each additional book.

Shipping & Handling _____

Texas residents add 8.25% sales tax _____

TOTAL ENCLOSED_____

check _____ or credit card # _____ exp. date_____

(Visa, MasterCard, Discover, American Express accepted)

Name _____

Address _____ Phone _____

City _____ State _____ Zip _____

**For postal address, phone number, fax number, email address
and other ways to order from Hannibal Books, see page 175.**